Tell me more...

The Ultimate Guide To Crafting & Delivering Inspiring Presentations Fearlessly

DAVID W KOLAKOWSKI

ISBN# 978-0-578-33173-7

DEDICATION

This book is dedicated to all those that have come before me and after me that stand in front of an audience that lack confidence, preparation, and skills to be able to enjoy the experience.

Kathy,
Thanks for your excellent presentation. Messaging & Presentation are the key to SMB success.

Good luck
[illegible signature]

Table of Contents

ABOUT THE AUTHOR

David Kolakowski has gone from dreading the very thought of standing in front of an audience to reveling in the excitement of it. He has been at the level of stress that most people have at some time in their career when it comes to standing in front of a group and has overcome it. He is just not another speaker. His performances are informative, entertaining and most of all remembered.

How did he get from stress to fun? The thought that presentations did not have to hurt began when he was preparing slides for another individual. He was asked to prepare 60 graphs and charts for a business presentation for an associate. Based upon what the graphs displayed, the speaker determined what he was going to say in the speech. As David observed the resulting presentation, he noticed that the slides were the dominant part of the presentation and the speaker appeared simply as a narrator, glued to the podium, motionless, emotionless, sweating, in a monotone, with the audience half asleep. There must be a better way.

From there David attended one two-day seminar on presentation skills, and a one-day seminar on presenting charts and graphs effectively. Both seminars had great information and were instrumental in his development. But neither seminar alone had the complete answers he was looking for.

Over the next two years, he watched over 200 presentations from various people and organizations and noted what he liked and disliked, what worked and what did not. He was tired of seeing speakers apologize for something that should not have happened, waiting through equipment glitches, speakers who did not make their point, and seeing stressed out and nervous speakers. He simply asked himself what he wanted to see and hear as a member of the audience.

Then came the epiphany. David was asked by his boss to attend and observe a series of presentations over a two-day period in Canada at an annual sales summit the company conducted. The purpose of his presence was to critique and provide an outline for training for improving the speakers so the next year's two-day summit would be better. The morning of the first day, he met for breakfast with the general manager of the operations and the corresponding Vice President with oversight responsibility for that division. Suddenly, he learned that there was no agenda, no planned speakers and no outline for the event and they turned to David and asked him if he would facilitate the entire two-day meeting. They said they wanted a facilitator to be someone that was not upper management from corporate. After nearly choking on a piece of bacon, he said, "Sure give me an hour."

Nobody should ever have people fly in from all over the country to attend a two-day event and not have a concrete slate of totally prepared speakers and sessions ready to go. Without having much time to prepare, David knew the best way to be effective, on such short notice, was to make it highly interactive. After his introduction and attention, grabbing hook, he proceeded to solicit responses from the audience in a working like session. He started out using a flip chart asking: What are our competitors offering that we are not and should be? Are we adequately represented in the relevant markets? Then he continued, what advantages do our products have in the marketplace? When you ask the sales reps what the company's weaknesses are, they will get very active and participate willingly. They filled up several flip charts and put them around the wall in the conference center. After lunch they broke out into groups and were given group tasks to come up with a wish list of items, they wanted to see corporate get behind in either enhancing the current products or expanding the product line. Towards the end of the first day each group made a presentation to management on their recommendations. It ended up being a very productive meeting and David realized that getting the audience involved makes presentations more enjoyable for the audience and reduces the preparation time, especially if there is no time to prepare. This was an addition to his notes.

After completing his notes on ways to improve presentations, David put them into action, trying out various techniques, keeping in mind the audience's perspective. He conducted several presentations, some up to two hours in length, before several hundred people. He has refined his approach and includes it here in this book to be shared with others. From being petrified to stand in front of a group of any size for a short 2-minute introduction to being thrilled at being asked to expand a one-hour presentation into 2 hours, the techniques applied in this book worked for David and will work for you.

David Kolakowski was born in Hartford, Connecticut and graduated from the University of Connecticut, with a bachelor's degree in business administration. He worked as a Certified Public Accountant for a Big Four accounting firm for nine years. He then went out on his own as a consultant, helping companies and individuals' better structure their business presentations, among other things. David has accumulated dozens of online video training modules to be shared with the world located at PresentationFormula.com. He now lives and works in Ocean, New Jersey, conducting and enjoying the presentations he makes.

1. INTRODUCTION

"There are always three speeches, for everyone you actually gave. The one you practiced, the one you gave, and the one you wish you gave." – Dale Carnegie

Why is it that so many people are scared to death to make a presentation? Why is it that most people look forward to a presentation's completion rather than to the presentation itself? Because presentations put people in the spotlight in front of a group and, due to fear or other reasons, people treat communication to a group differently than one-to-one conversations.

The word "Fun" and the concept of "Conquering the Audience!" generally are not thoughts of people who are giving presentations. Otherwise, they would have a better attitude toward their presentation. In trying to convince someone or a group of someones to your way of thinking, "Attitude" is your most important asset. If you are unsure of yourself, motionless, emotionless, not focused on your point or nervous trying to make your point, you will not win many people over to your way of thinking. But if you are confident, projecting a positive self-image, organized and full of emotion and passion, the people you are speaking to will be convinced that you believe in your topic. And you will have a better chance of winning them over to your side.

Part of the reason for the uncomfortable feeling relating to making a presentation is a lack of training. I am not referring to technical training. If you are making a presentation, you are likely regarded as a technical expert on your topic. It is presentation training that most speakers lack. Presentation training is not as difficult or complicated as one would imagine. It is more an undoing of bad habits that detract from a presentation than learning difficult presentation skills. The mere fear of being embarrassed and acting out of line in front of a group has set the stage for being motionless, monotone and conservative in front of a group.

Think for a moment: If you are trying to convince someone in a one-on-one conversation of your point of view, you would probably use significant voice inflection, change speed in your speech pattern, add good hand and arm movement and demonstrate some strong body language. If you do not convince the person to your side after expressing yourself strongly, at least he or she will be convinced that you strongly believe in your position. This is a natural style of speaking.

Why then, do people stand in front of an audience in a formal presentation and throw out all the important forms of communication, except the words? Why do they stand motionless and speak in a monotone voice? This is truly unnatural communication. Being natural in your communications is fun and easy. But being unnatural, trying to communicate without using all your communications tools, is difficult. Being in an unnatural position or a fearful state of mind is what makes the presentation such a dreadful experience. Words are important but the other aspects of communication, the ones that show your confidence and convictions, are the ones that allow you to conquer the audience and have fun in the process. If up to 90% of communication is nonverbal, to be successful you must incorporate these more convincing nonverbal tools.

Moreover, if you deliver an unnatural, monotone, uninspiring presentation, chances are it will not be memorable. You are making a presentation so that others remember what you said, understand your position and act on your recommendation. They will not follow up if they cannot even remember your presentation. If you are giving a short one-to-two-minute introduction, you must be creative to be memorable. You have a limited amount of time to establish credibility, so you need to make the most of it, and quickly.

Speaking in a front of a group is a learnable skill. This book addresses the discomfort experienced by speakers in preparing for and giving a presentation to a group. It explains how you can prepare yourself, so you turn your attitude from one of looking forward to the completion of your presentation, to looking forward to performing your presentation. It shows how to develop and coordinate your content, so the audience walks away with what you want them to. It explains how to create and use visual aids effectively - what works and what does not. It will reacquaint you with the natural forms of communication and show you how to use them to your advantage in your presentation. And most of all, it will help you to have fun in the process. The chapters of this book focus on the commonsense aspects of communication techniques that will raise the level of any presentation and be memorable.

2. TELL ME MORE

"Storytelling offers the opportunity to talk with your audience, not at them." – Laura Holloway

The concept of "Tell me more" was derived after watching hundreds of presentations both long and short, and analyzing why many of them were very difficult to watch. The ones that were difficult lacked a storyline or a theme. I kept finding myself saying "Where is this presentation going?" And the short one-to-two-minute mini-introductions, were generally uninformative. I discovered the "Tell me more" concept after understanding how the brain works, specifically how people react to certain words and phrases. We will delve into the brain in a later chapter. Essentially, the goal of the presenter is to spark and keep the audience's interest. Create intrigue and mystery, using one sentence to create interest and anticipation for your next sentence, so the audience is literally waiting for your next syllable. When you speak there are generally two different types of responses you will get. They are either interested in what you said, or they are not. The people that are not interested fall into what I call the "So What" or "Who Cares" category. In the "So What' or "Who Cares" category, each time something comes out of your mouth they fail to connect or understand so their brains turn you off as their bodies screams "So What" and "Who cares." This is not the response you are looking for from your audience.

To move your audience to the interested category, you need to structure your statements in a way that leads them on, so they want to hear more. You want them on the edge of their seats begging to hear your next line. This is what I refer to as the "Tell me more" strategy. Each sentence you speak, you want your audience to think "Hmm, that's interesting. Tell me more." For example, say you are making a presentation about how your company acquired a logistics company to deliver its products to its customers, so they don't have to rely on the main carriers. You could just tell them exactly that, or you can lead them on. Create some intrigue. Be creative and maybe start with "Last week we had an incredible breakthrough for our company." Now the audience is interested, and everyone is thinking "Tell me more." Then you outline the issues you had in the past with your delivery and the resulting increase in customer support inquiries and negative reviews. All the heads would be nodding at this point. You then talk about the different ways that this problem could be solved that was considered. This engages the audience's brain to subconsciously sense their feedback as to the options that were considered. All this time the audience is glued to your every word waiting for you to "Tell me more" and get to that incredible breakthrough. Each sentence provides more information and builds on the excitement and anticipation as you get closer to the announcement, until you finally get there. You can either tell them or lead them by engaging them through a thought process and use a story to deliver your content.

The comparison to "Tell me more" and the "So What" or "Who Cares" response can best be illustrated using a typical short networking event type of introduction. For some reason, in the distant past someone suggested a style for these types of introductions that guarantees that no one will remember what you said. This standard introduction says to state your name, your company name, what you do or your title, what your company does, brag about yourself or your company, state your name again and then sit down. If we break down that introduction, it is full of "So What" statements and there is nothing that creates that "Tell me more" intrigue. What is the purpose of stating your name if you are not famous or they don't know how you can help them? No one really cares about your company name, your job title or your name until they know how they can benefit from your products or services. Then people tend to brag about themselves or their company saying things like "I have been doing this for 30 years" or "Our company is the largest supplier in the country." Bragging does not connect with the audience and most people will think "Who Cares" when someone starts bragging about their company or business. In my experience, in the networking events I have been to where they do introductions, 95% of all introductions follow this incorrect approach. The result is that 95% of the people are not remembered.

So, what does work? Stop bragging and stop saying things that no one cares about. Talk about things that directly benefit your customers and make it so the audience can relate. For example, if you are a financial advisor, you could start your introduction by saying "Last year our clients earned 20% more than the market." Everyone in the audience will sit up and think "Wow, I want that. Tell me more." The next sentence to follow that would be a little more information about how the process is different and is geared for the benefit of the clients. Now you have their interest and as you keep adding more information, you keep getting the "Tell me more" response on their faces, until you get to the end when you tell them your company and your name and how they can contact you. Design your introduction so that it tells a story, leads them down a path, strategically, and gets them to want to talk to you, and hopefully hire you. Alternatively, if you are a financial advisor, you could go back to telling people how big your company is and how long you have been with the firm, how many assets your company manages, etc. But that is not going to make you stand out, it is not going to connect with your audience and will result in you not being remember and not generating a slew of people wanting to hire you.

Throughout the rest of this book, keep in mind this "Tell me more" concept. The concept of telling a story and leading them down that path, showing them you have what it takes to solve their problem or make them understand the action you want them to take.

3. UNDERSTANDING YOUR AUDIENCE

"People will forget what you said, people will forget what you did, but people will never forget how you made them feel." -- Maya Angelou

The art of communication is not merely speaking, it's getting others to hear your message and act on what you say. So often, people get up in front of a room and just start speaking without regard to their audiences; how their audience perceives them and what's going on inside their brains. Understanding who is in your audience, why they came out to hear you speak and how their brains work will go a long way in making your presentation a lot easier for you and your audience. In this chapter we address how to determine who is in your audience and what their expectations are and why they are in your audience. Additionally, we address some of the physiological attributes of the brain to get a better understanding of how your message is being received by your audience.

Who is in Your Audience?

If the person does not speak your language, they won't understand a single thing you said. If your audience is a group of technology novices, and your presentation is on blockchain and crypto currencies, they will have no idea what you are talking about. As a result, no one will respond to your call to action. Similarly, if you dumb down your presentation to accommodate all levels of people, no one will be interested in what you have to say.

You must first understand who is in your audience and what is their relationship to you. Your audience could be internal corporate people both above you and below you or your peers, customers, prospects, friends, competitors, investors, and supporters. Each group may have a different objective of why they are there, and what they want to get out of your presentation. Similarly, you may have a different call to action for each of these groups because of their relationship to you. Sometimes internal audiences are not sure why they are there, so it is up to you to educate and inform them, and then get them to act.

Internal Corporate Audiences

Let's look at the first group, your internal organization audience. If you are doing a corporate presentation or training inside your organization, your message is completely different than if you are presenting to customers or prospects. Generally, internal presentations are either training or information related. You are either providing information on the latest happenings at the company, the financial results of the most recent period, a new acquisition, a new product line, a new hire, a new computer system, project status meetings, etc. The presentation's goal to this audience is to inform and educate. Some things may be more interesting to your internal audience than other things. Employees may not be as interested in the financial results of the company as they would be in an announcement of a new incentive compensation plan.

Beware, changing the status quo is a risk. People get antsy when things change. If you are announcing a new hire, people begin thinking, if they are going to restructure the organization I wonder if my job is at risk. Similarly, for a new computer system, they think, "Will this computer system replace my job. Even financial results can be scary to employees – for bad results, they wonder if their jobs will be cut and for good results they wonder if the company may be acquired. Try to anticipate how your audience might react and be ready for it. Focusing on professionalism and quality is key as it might mean the difference between a promotion and job stagnation.

Presentations inside your organization are still much lower risk than presentations to prospects, customers, or potential investors. A bad presentation sending the wrong message can have a negative financial impact on the company as a whole, and if you're the one making that presentation, you might experience some negative consequences as well.

External Presentations

When you make a presentation to a group outside your own organization, the risk is high, as it could result in a lost client, lost revenue, lost funding, or some other lost opportunity. Often, the external presentation is a one-time deal. You make a presentation and you either get the sale, keep the client, get the funding, secure the opportunity or you do not. When presenting internally to your organization, often it is informational, and a failed presentation would not have such a drastic effect on the organization.

Modifying Your Presentation to Your Audience

Regardless of who your audience is you must take the following steps to understand who you are speaking in front of. It is your job to do the research to get the demographic information beforehand which will also help you structure your presentation accordingly. Consider the following key demographic data to adjust your presentation:

1) **Education Level** – you should first assess the makeup of your audience's educational background. If you are speaking to college graduates and postgraduate degreed people you need to consider that when you're preparing your content. Talking over or under your

audience's education level will not win you favor. The well-educated will think you are patronizing them if you use simple language and speaking over the heads of a less educated audience will fall on deaf ears. Neither will result in a successful presentation.

2) **Job Level** – If you are making a presentation to the board of directors or upper management of a company, they would expect you to deliver a highly professional and impactful presentation. This is where you can really shine with your presentation skills - you need to speak their language at a level they expect. Speaking to the board of directors or to upper management, they would expect one form of language, but if you are making a presentation to the labor force that works in the warehouse, you must speak a language that they would understand. While a board and upper management might know what EBITA and pro forma mean, the labor force would probably have no idea. Understand that the reason each group is there is completely different as well as what you expect them to do because of your presentation.

3) **Income Level** – the next category to consider is their income level. Are you presenting to a group of very wealthy individuals, or are you presenting to a group of middle-class individuals or are you addressing a lower-income crowd? Each group has different needs, wants and desires listening to you speak. For example, a politician may want to hand out goodies to certain groups while also catering to his big fat cat donors. That is a fine line to walk. One group may be looking for investing strategies for maximizing their retirement and minimizing their tax burden, while another group may be looking for ways to cut costs to be able to pay their bills tomorrow.

4) **Audience Knowledge** – It is important to understand the knowledge level of your audience. This is different from education level and may even be more important. You do not want to cover some basic concepts that the audience already knows, for fear of losing their interest, but you also don't want to talk over their knowledge level, since they will not be able to follow you. No one will love your presentation if they do not understand it. To be safe, cover some of the basic points in the beginning so you can set a knowledge baseline for your presentation. The people that know the subject will accept a short refresher while the novices in the room will appreciate the education. A second facet of the knowledge issue is to try to assess the perspective of your audience on your topic. If you are proposing a strategy for the company, it is advisable to get some sense of their appetite for this strategy beforehand so you can address their attitude in

your points. For example, if you are proposing a new computer system, and the audience is ready to accept a new system because of the failed current system, they will react differently than an audience that thinks the current system is fine. It is important to match the knowledge level of the audience with the relevant information that they need to know. Do not go into the extraneous details of how we got to a certain point or how the problem arose if they just want to know where we are going next and how you plan to solve the problem.

5) **Cultural Background** – In this age of hypersensitivity, it is important to consider your audience. If you have a diverse audience, make sure you use examples representing different groups. This includes using different images in your presentation to demonstrate your sensitivity to diversity.

6) **Age and Gender** – Age and gender presents some interesting challenges. Different generations use different words for the same thing. Elder audiences may be more interested in understanding how they will retire without financial worry, while younger audiences may be more interested in their current career opportunities. A predominantly male audience will react differently to your presentation than a predominantly female audience. Try to think about these different perspectives when preparing your presentation and consider getting some feedback from the opposite of you.

7) **Other Demographics** – other demographic data that you may need to pull together to get a good understanding of your audience includes geographic location, race, religion, marital status, homeownership status, and anything else that is relevant to your presentation.

The Audience's Expertise

Another audience consideration is their expertise:

1) **Technical Versus Creative** – If you are working with a team to create the company website, you first must have the business marketing leaders define the overall objective of the website and the graphical look they want to convey, in essence, the message and the professional look and feel. Those discussions with the marketing team can take weeks or months before one piece of code is written. Bringing in the techno specialists in this marketing phase is generally a bad idea. It would be difficult to balance the creative flow of energy from marketing types with the discussion of what technology will be involved. I have seen meetings where the technology people kept

interrupting about technology requirements and security issues while the marketing objectives are not even set. This makes for a difficult and impossible situation. Make sure to have the right people in the meeting at the right time to avoid this type of confusion.

2) **Production Versus Administrative** – They both approach their day with getting things done, but that is probably where the similarities end. Production employees may have issues with production line safety, staffing levels by station, cleanliness, and supervision, where administrative office workers are more focused on completing paperwork and office related tasks.

3) **Sales Versus Support** – Sales and support have different mindsets and attitude differences. True sales are about landing the client and moving on and letting customer support deal with the implementation, delivery and follow up issues. Customer support presentations should focus more on process and client satisfaction, while sales presentations should focus on getting more leads in the pipeline.

4) **Hunters Versus Farmers** – Taking the sales force to the next step is differentiating between hunters and farmers. Hunters are the ones that go and find the new clients and farmers are the ones that take those new clients and manage the relationship and upsell new products. Farmers are more like customer service reps. They try to keep the client happy and want to find ways to satisfy them, so they buy more stuff. Hunters are typically just looking for that next big lead. Their attitude and patience are completely different.

Regardless of the group, they all listen for different things and want to get different things out of your presentation. You must keep this in mind.

Where Are They on the Maslow's Needs Hierarchy?

What level are they on Maslow's Needs Hierarchy? If you adequately research your audience, try to discern where they stand on Maslow's Needs Hierarchy. If you are preaching Self Actualization to an audience that is looking to secure economic safety, your speech

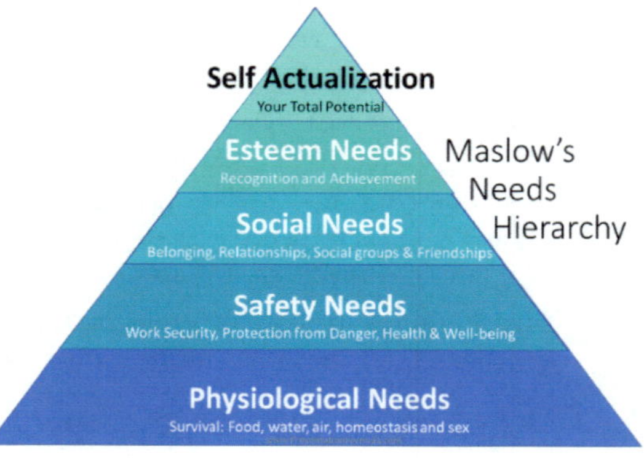

will fall on deaf ears. I remember a speaker talking to an audience of people trying to make ends meet, and his theme was giving back to the community. He was talking about taking some of your earnings and doing good things with it, helping the community improve. Well, that is all well and good, but most of the people in that room were just looking for a way to pay their own bills and keep their house without going into default. Remember these levels when you research your audience. Make sure not to talk over your audiences' level or beneath them. I see a lot of programs that dangle the "You too can be rich" scheme and achieve high recognition, without having a real roadmap for the audience members. The calls to action simply end up being to buy something from the speaker. Don't be like that.

Different Types of Learners

Your audience will be a collection of different individuals with different backgrounds, perspectives, and experiences. There will also be different types of learners that you will have to address. There are three types of learners, visual, auditory, and kinesthetic. Not everyone in your audience will be one type of another, there will be a mixture. You must consider this when preparing your presentation.

Visual Learners

Visual learners learn best with pictures and visualization. They look around and examine the situation. They may stare when angry and beam when happy. Facial expression is a good indicator of emotions in the visual learner. They think in pictures and details and have vivid imaginations. When extensive listening is required, they may be quiet and become impatient. Neat in appearance, they may dress in the same manner all the time.

Visual learners have greater immediate recall of words that are presented visually. Visual learners like to take notes. Relatively unaware of sounds, they can be distracted by visual disorder or movement. They solve problems deliberately, planning and organizing their thoughts by writing them down. They like to read descriptions and narratives.

To connect with visual learners use seeing words that describe things like, text, slides, pictures, graphics, outlines, charts, diagrams, lists, notes. Use words like illustrate, show, outline, label or see. 65% of all people of visual learners. Visual learners take good notes and begin to look around if you are losing their interest.

Auditory Learners

Auditory learners are good at remembering conversations, also they are good presenters. They talk about what to do, about the pros and cons of a situation. They indicate emotion through the tone, pitch, and volume of their voices. They enjoy listening but cannot wait to get their chance to talk. They tend toward long and repetitive descriptions. They like hearing themselves and others talk.

Auditory learners tend to remember names but forget faces and are easily distracted by sounds. They enjoy reading dialogue and plays and dislike lengthy narratives and descriptions. Auditory learners benefit from oral instruction. They prefer to hear or recite information and benefit from auditory repetition. To accommodate your auditory learners in your audience, use the words like "explain, describe, discuss, and state." Auditory learners may have difficulty interpreting charts and graphs. 30% of all people are auditory learners.

Kinesthetic Learners

Kinesthetic learners like to try things out, touch, feel and manipulate objects. Their body tension is a good indication of their emotions. They gesture when speaking, are poor listeners, stand very close when speaking or listening, and quickly lose interest in long dissertation. They remember best what has been done, not what they have seen or talked about. They prefer direct involvement in what they are learning. They are distractible and find it difficult to pay attention to auditory or visual presentations. Rarely an avid reader, they may fidget frequently while handling a book. Often poor spellers, they need to write down words to determine if they "feel" right. Kinesthetic learning takes place when your audience participates in physical activities rather than listening are watching a presentation. Luckily only 5 % of learners are kinesthetic learners. Use words like feel, rough, smooth, bumpy, grit, etc. when trying to appeal to these learners.

Logistic Issues with Learner types

It may seem like you are repeating yourself multiple times to get your point across, but repetition is the best way to get your point across. Think of it this way. One third of your audience is blind and will listen to the words you say to get them to understand. Almost two thirds are deaf and need you to paint them a picture to get your point across. And a fraction will be both deaf and blind and will need to feel your concept. A nice graphic would appeal to the visual learners but follow it up with some nice prose and use some touchy feeling words and you will cover all bases and make a connection with all three learner types.

Why They Came to Hear You Speak

Once have done your research and gathered and all the information about your potential audience, the next step is to identify the potential pain points. What is your audience struggling with? If they are looking to solve problems, once you understand their pain and suffering, or what they fear they might experience, you can tailor your presentation to provide solutions to solve these problems and alleviate those fears.

Prospects want to hear you speak to see if your products or services can solve a problem they have. Management may be seeking information to help them make some decisions. Employees may be interested in learning about new benefits. If you are giving a eulogy or a wedding toast, the audience is looking to hear some emotional stories, that only you can provide.

How your Audience Listens

In order to deliver an effective presentation, you must not only understand what your audience expects to get out of your presentation, but you must understand how your audience listens. This means you must know the science behind listening. How the brain works and how it receives stimuli, particularly your message and your presentation.

Decisions and Emotions

Several studies (see one study at https://brandaura.com/emotion-science-research/) have concluded that approximately 90% of all decisions made every single day are based on emotions rather than rational, logical thought. You may think otherwise but you're just kidding yourself. And after making an emotional decision, immediately afterwards it is followed up with a logic rationalization of why we came to that conclusion. You may sit with a pen and paper to create your wish list and jot down all the logical requirements for your next car purchase. For example, you want 4 doors with a back seat for the kids and the dog, a sizeable trunk for your gear and luggage, good gas mileage, with limited expensive extras. Then what happens? You go down to the dealer and the next thing you know you drive away with a car that has strayed from your wish list. As you drive away you immediately start rationalizing your decision; I don't really need such a big trunk, I don't want to lug all that stuff around. Why do I need back seats? We'll leave the kids with Grandma? I know the mileage is not great, but gas is cheap. And this goes on until your rational brain is satisfied that your emotional decision was justified.

This works on a smaller scale too. You may be out late at night and need some food, so you go into a diner on the side of the road. Most of these diners have 10+ page menus. Your logical brain is reading item after item after item trying to decide, narrowing down your selections to your usual choices. But your logical brain cannot make your ultimate decision. Should I eat off the breakfast menu? How about the lunch menu? Maybe I should have a steak? Oh, I should probably go for the salad and watch my waistline. The rational brain is processing all the facts and information and is incapable of deciding until your emotions come into play. Maybe the waitress comes over and describes the specials or the menu has a nice picture of something that your brain connects to. The specials may include an appetizer, an entrée and dessert and all for an enticing special price. Suddenly, in an instant your emotions kick in and you order the special. Even if it goes against your rational analysis of the menu from a minute earlier. And after you order what do you do? You rationalize your decision. I have been good on my diet this week, so splurging on this one meal won't hurt. I will run an extra mile tomorrow. I won't eat meat for the next two weeks. Our brain goes on and on until we rationalize enough so we convinced ourselves the decision was right.

I remember reading a study where they sampled people that suffered from a disease that prevented their brain's capability to use emotions. These people were incapable of expressing regret, remorse or sympathy and they were also incapable of making very simple decisions. The study presented the group with incredibly detailed list of facts of alternative scenarios. While each correct answer was obvious, they were unable to pick the right one because of their lack of emotions. The facts were blatant, and the answers were easy, but without having any emotions, they ended up merely guessing. Where do you find such individuals with no regret, no remorse, and no sympathy? The answer is on death row in prison because they are psychopaths. Hopefully, these people will not be in your audience when you are speaking. Your audience will have emotions and will be able to make decisions. Knowing that people buy and make other decisions based on emotions, you must focus your presentation to tap into those emotions, make that connection and get them to act in a way you want.

The Amygdala – The Prehistoric Brain

"It is not failure itself that holds you back; it is the fear of failure that paralyzes you." – Brian Tracy

The dictionary defines the amygdala as an almond shaped mass of gray matter inside each cerebral hemisphere involved with the experiencing of all emotions. The amygdala is part of the limbic system, which is a neural network that mediates many aspects of emotion and memory. The amygdala analyses thousands of pieces of information all daylong and is responsible for assessing danger. It offers three responses to danger: fight, flight or freeze.

The amygdala is often referred to as the prehistoric or lizard brain because it is the one part of the body that has never evolved since the beginning of mankind. It is the main reason why so many people are afraid to speak in front of an audience. The amygdala is incapable of discerning the difference between the fear presented by coming face-to-face with a saber tooth tiger and the fear of speaking and standing in front of an audience giving a presentation.

Fear comes from the unknown. As the amygdala is scanning your surroundings constantly, it is trying to analyze every object to determine if danger exists. It uses its memory to match up whatever it senses to determine if something is dangerous. If it looks around the room, it sees a clock. It knows from its memory that clocks are safe. And it proceeds to the next item to process. Sometimes it comes across something that connects with a bad memory and forces the body to act a different way. For example, if when you were a kid and you walked through the park and you got beat up by the neighborhood bully, chances are when you see another park it is going stir up that old memory. As a result, you may you take a different route rather than walking through the park, or at least you will be on high alert when going through the park.

When something is unknown the amygdala focuses on the object longer until it can discern the threat it presents. When you speak in front of a group the result is unknown. This can be good, and it can be bad. It can be good because the audience will focus on you at first and keep focusing as long as you maintain their interest and curiosity. It can be bad if you prove to them that you are not a threat, not interesting and not worth paying attention to.

The audience response is unknown. That creates fear. Unfortunately, that fear creates a fight or flight or freeze response, and since you can't fight or flight when you are supposed to present, speakers often freeze. This freezing presents itself in monotone, quiet talk, stiff movement, a tightening of the vocalcords and emotionless rhetoric. This response is exactly the opposite of what you need to eliminate the fear in the first place. You need a dynamic voice, active movement across the stage, a relaxed set of vocal cords and a speech full of emotion.

That is what the amygdala is doing in the speaker's brain, but what about the audience's brain and their amygdala? The audience showed up to see the speaker talk about a specific topic that interested them. They are looking forward to gaining knowledge and information to help them better their lives or their businesses or their relationships or their diets or whatever. They think you are the expert and will impart that knowledge to them. However, before anything starts, they look at you with a little fear of the unknown. They probably read some information in advance about your background from the conference guide or short biography to know why you are the expert and why you are speaking in front of them. It is your job to make sure that you live up to that expectation and maintain your credibility.

The audiences' amygdalas are looking for something that you say or do to connect with their memory so they can either write you off, shut you down or accept you. Think of a shiny object. The eye typically is attracted to a shiny shimmering object off in the distance. The eye becomes mesmerized by this shiny object. It maintains focus on that object until it ceases to interest them, whether that is because it has determined it is not something to fear or it cannot help them. Your goal as speaker is to create a presentation that creates that same shiny object response, to keep them focusing on you and your subject all the way through to the end.

In the remainder of this book, we will address how to create this interest, that shiny object, to keep the attention of your audience so they don't lose focus and you don't jeopardize your credibility and expert status. You will make them feel that they are getting every bit out of what they expected to get out of your presentation.

The Danger of Stereotyping Yourself

One of the ways to damage your credibility is to stereotype yourself. Stereotyping yourself simply means giving yourself a label that the audiences immediately relate to something in their memory. This can be a bad memory or a good memory. You cannot know. If you tell someone you are a contractor, you don't know whether they had some work done on their house previously by a contractor that did an excellent job or if the contractor they used walked off the job and left a mess behind. For this reason, you should stay away from labeling yourself up front. If you stood and said you are a used car salesman, it doesn't matter if you're the most compassionate, nice, intelligent used car salesman in the world, their brain is immediately going to associate you with some of their other past experiences they may have had with a used car salesman as well as the existing stereotype. Once the brain pigeonholes you into a specific stereotype it is difficult to pry your way out from that hole. And at that point, getting anyone to listen to your presentation may be difficult. I must walk that line as well. If I ever lead with "I spent 10 years working in finance and accounting as a CPA," most people will write me off as an accountant. At a networking event as I was talking to someone, he looked at my business card and said, "I have an accountant," and he just walked away. At the same event, I put my business cards in my pocket, and I talked to another attendee. I said what I did, not that I was just an accountant, and he asked if we could get together to discuss business. By giving the first person my business card, it stereotyped me into the typical accountant role and that person's amygdala shut down and he literally walked away. By me avoiding the stereotype with a second person the conversation continued and the follow-up and the business continued.

4. PREPARING FOR YOUR PRESENTATION

"Only the prepared speaker deserves to be confident."
– Dale Carnegie

You have been chosen or you volunteered to give a presentation. You are lucky, even though you may not realize it. You have an opportunity to show your expertise and wow your audience. This has the possibility of raising your stock with your employer and increasing your reputation to your audience. For some reason you have been deemed the expert and the best person to make this presentation and it is now your chance to show them you deserved it. The last thing you want to do is stand in front of your audience unprepared and unorganized. You must take steps to make your presentation awesome and wow the crowd. This chapter will walk you through the steps to build the content for your presentation so you can do just that.

Incorporating The 5 E's

One of the ways to really stimulate your audiences' amygdala into your presentation and is to incorporate the five E's. Emotion, Education, Enthusiasm, Entertainment and Engagement. If you're trying to present to a crowd and you don't have at least one of these five E's, then you are going to fail. The more E's you can incorporate into your presentation the better off you will be. Certain presentations are not appropriate for certain E's, of course. For example, giving a financial presentation you may stay clear of the entertainment and maybe dial it back a little on the enthusiasm factor. Let us take a closer look at each one of these:

Emotions – as a discussed earlier, 90% of all decisions are made based on emotions, and later justified with rationale. Similarly, you must incorporate emotions into your presentation to make the connection with your audience. Nobody wants to sit in an audience and hear someone ramble off a logical list of products and services and accomplishments. Unless you are holding a puppy while you are speaking you must find another way to create an emotional connection. The best way to make an emotional connection is by telling a story. In the later chapter we address how to take your audience on a magical journey by telling them a captivating story and connecting emotionally with your audience to make your presentation successful. Emotions are the most important E and must be incorporated into every successful presentation. Even in financial presentations, creating a story including some personal challenges and experiences to support the numbers, will improve your presentation. If you are presenting unemotional facts and figures, you might as well just email it to your audience.

Enthusiasm – You are the expert. You better be very passionate about your topic, otherwise why would anyone in your audience become excited if you are not showing enthusiasm? Nobody in the audience wants to sit there and watch and listen to a stick person lacking passion and excitement make a presentation. Bring your passion and your enthusiasm and you will be successful. Enthusiasm will not come out naturally unless you practice it. If you must, make notes and other cues to emphasis where you need to stress some points with a higher level of enthusiasm.

"The energy level of the audience is the same as the speaker's. For better...or for worse." – Andras Baneth

Entertainment – Entertainment falls into the 3 E's category but is probably the one item that is the most difficult to bring to bear, especially if you are not a natural entertainer. However, if you are telling an emotional story and you bring in that passion and create an emotional connection, then technically you are entertaining them. If you are educating them and providing some creative learning techniques, technically you are entertaining them. It is a fine line, and if your presentation lacks enthusiasm, you will not be entertaining them. But be careful, don't go out of your way to incorporate humor or other forms of entertainment if it's not appropriate for the topic at hand or if you are not good at it. Entertainment must also be rehearsed before delivering your presentation. One of the secrets of entertaining is to tie everything together, using the underlying theme of your presentation. Comedians often do this when they start with a series of topics and then at the end, they bring back the main topic as they close the show. When you conclude your story and it ties your entire presentation together, it is a true art form of entertainment, but also gives the audience a sense that they got what they expected. Typically, if you do it right, you will be followed with applause.

"Once you get people laughing, they're listening, and you can tell them almost anything." – Herbert Gardner

Education – people love to learn. Providing a great learning and educational seminar and speaking event is a great way to connect to your audience. Even if you're providing a non-educational presentation, it is always great to incorporate bits of information and knowledge that they didn't expect to get. For example, if you are giving a talk on the environment or overpopulation, providing facts like: "97% of the people live on 3% of the land," or "The average person commutes for 53 minutes every day and if they work for 45 years, they will ultimately spend 8,745 hours, or an entire full year sitting in their car, bus or train." Stating facts like this, creates credibility, but more importantly, makes your audience think. If your audience starts to think "Maybe, we should not live so close together." Or "Maybe we should consider telecommuting more." This type of education really gets your audience engaged.

Engagement – Engaging the audience involves giving them a reason to listen and getting them to keep listening. It goes beyond just telling the story, it goes beyond educating them, it goes beyond entertaining them, it is connecting with the heart and soul of your audience. There are several ways to accomplish this as follows:

- Share a personal experience – people love to hear your personal experiences, especially if you can elaborate on something you failed at, overcame and then moved on. People can really relate to that type of personal story.

- Ask questions of the audience – Just like in high school, when the teacher asked a question, the entire class suddenly started paying attention again. Even if it is just a rhetorical question, ask questions and keep their brains functioning at full speed.

- State some facts that cause your audience to think – As I mentioned in the Education E above, this is great way to engage your audience.

- Post a provocative or controversial question and statement – As I mentioned above in the Education section, after you post some facts, you can follow up with some provocative questions, like: "Wouldn't it be better if we all did not live in densely populated areas?" Or "What is on the other 97% of the land that we don't live on?" It engages their brains and makes them want to participate.

- Provide anecdotes throughout your presentation – Stories and real-life events that support your topics are key in making your points or supporting your ideas. Without anecdotes, your presentation may seem stiff and sterile.

- Tie in your topic to the previous speakers at the same event – It is a good idea to find out what other people are going to speak about before you. You do not want to make a presentation that contradicts your previous speaker. If you can tie your speech into what your previous speaker talked about, it not only creates credibility and freshness in you, but validates the previous speaker as well. I once presented last in an environmental series of presentations. The speakers before me talked about how to mix cement while emitting less CO2 by 10%, and another talked about how to stage the forms to speed the curing process of the cement. I had to act swiftly to adjust my presentation to incorporate those themes as I discussed using components in the mixing process to eliminate the emission of CO2 in the mixing process and was ideal for use in forms to aid in the speed of the curing process. While I had never met the other two speakers prior to that day, I was still able to incorporate their ideas in my presentation. Afterwards, the audience considered me an expert and thought that I had previously been working with those other two speakers.

- Connect your presentation to a current event (the more current the better). Just as telling an old joke can convince your audience that the rest of the presentation is old and outdated. Starting your presentation by incorporating current events make it look fresh and current and will convince your audience that the rest of your presentation is also fresh and current. I typically try to get up extra early in the morning of the presentation and watch the news, and read the paper, looking for stories that I can incorporate into the presentation for that day. Typically, at a meeting that starts at 8 am, I will probably be the only one that has seen those stories. I educate them and at the same time I create more credibility for my presentation.

- Build in more audience involvement – Audience involved can take on several different forms. Some fitness people use tricks to get people out of their seats to do some stretching or other physical activities. Other more cerebral presentations will hand out worksheets to get the audience to jot down some answers to some questions to be later used in the meat of the presentation. There are other techniques to create break out groups to get teams to work together to solve problems and other ways to have volunteers to come to the front. Whatever you do, make sure it is relevant to your presentation topic.

Taking Your Audience on a Magical Journey

A good speech requires a topic that others want to learn about and since you have the requisite expertise you have been chosen to speak about it. Once you have your topic, you must build your story around it. The story personalizes it. This story and how it is presented is how you take your audience along with you on a presentation journey. Deciding on the right approach and story depends on your audience, their knowledge and expertise level, as well as their expectations. People love to be intrigued by and listen to stories. As the puppet master, you should guide them through the story, conveying your message and maintaining the attention of your audience. The journey needs to start with an intriguing thought that captures the audience, creating the "Tell me more" response. Once you have raised their interest, taking the audience along with you on the rest of your journey is easy. If you have piqued their interest well enough it will be a magical journey for both you and the audience. Sometimes, for data intensive presentations, it is difficult to develop a story, but be creative and your audience will appreciate it, remember it, and then act on your recommendation.

Getting Introduced to the Audience

When you stand in front of the audience and list your biography including schooling, past accomplishments and awards, the audience looks at that as bragging, and it puts you in an awkward position. The audience may despise you for bragging about yourself and suddenly you find you have dug a big hole that is difficult to get out of. But when someone else introduces you and lists your biography and accomplishments, it inspires the audience, raising their interest level and they will look forward to your presentation.

Write your own introduction, gear it to the audience and hand it to the person that will introduce you. Gear your introduction to the specific audience emphasizing those accomplishments that are more relevant to that audience. For example, when I speak in front of technology audiences, I focus more on some of my technology accomplishments, when I talk to a financial crowd, I will reference my extensive financial background, etc.

Avoiding the self-introduction frees you up to talk about your topic and jump right into your content, versus trying to justify why you are there and avoiding that awkward moment.

A typical introduction for me is as follows:

> "Our next speaker is originally from Connecticut, got his undergraduate degree in Business at the University of Connecticut, earned his CPA credentials at Deloitte & Touche, where he worked in Silicon Valley, working with start-ups and assisting them in raising venture capital of approximately $1 billion. He spent several years as an executive at a large insurance company before starting his own software company in 1998. He has won awards for 3 of his software

products and holds one patent and two trademarks." And then include something directly relevant to the topic of the presentation.

The audience will connect with something in your introduction that will immediately elicit the "Tell me more" response. For example, someone might hear that I worked in Silicon Valley with startups and the person might think; "Interesting, that's a perspective I want to hear more about."

Your Objective and Your Call to Action

Your objective of your presentation is synonymous with defining your call to action – What you want your audience to do as a result of your presentation. If you are making an internal presentation, whether it is training or information conveyance, your call to action may simply be acknowledgement and acceptance. If you are presenting financial results to management, they probably will either be satisfied with the presentation or ask for additional information or supporting information for specific items. If you are presenting changes to the employee benefits plans, your call to action would be to get them to read the plans and sign up and select their options online by a specific date. When you are presenting to potential new customers the ultimate call to action is to have them sign on the dotted line and close the sale, but short of that, getting them to move to the next step in the sales process is a more likely scenario. When presenting to bankers and investors, you want them to ask for your slide deck, a business plan or a financial statement and set up an appointment for a follow up or call back. Knowing the makeup of your audience, what your objective is, you now know what you must do. Start to organize your content to begin to build your presentation.

5. PRESENTATION CONTENT

"If you have an important point to make, don't try to be subtle or clever. Use a pile driver. Hit the point once. Then come back and hit it again. Then hit it a third time with a tremendous whack." -- Winston Churchill

It is contended that content is only 20% responsible for the overall success of a presentation. However, without strong content, you are just dancing in front of your audience.

Developing and organizing content is one of the most difficult tasks for speakers. Many spend most of their time on it, and more speakers stress over content than any other factor. Yet, after all that time preparing for and worrying about the content of a speech, poor content is usually the root cause of a poor presentation.

If content only counts for 20% of success, how can it have such a dramatic impact on the outcome? If you do not have a strong main theme, a good story, your presentation will simply not be remembered. Further, if your introduction is not full of thought-provoking content, you may never get your audience to engage in your topic. And if your slides or other graphic presentations are not directly tied to your main theme, they may distract from your presentation and confuse your audience.

Developing good content and establishing a strong main theme makes delivering the presentation much easier. Remember, you want to take your audience on a magical journey. One that they will always remember, so you must have a thought-provoking introduction that makes them yearn for you to "***Tell them more***." And having your main theme firmly identified will make it easier to create your slides, prepare your emphasis points, identify appropriate transitions, develop a thought-provoking introduction, and finish with an effective conclusion.

The Presentation Structure

Your presentation should have 3 distinct sections. Your Introduction, the Body or main content and the Closing. Each section has a unique and necessary job to do in making your presentation successful. We will cover what to include in each section. The best way to make a presentation is to structure it in the form of a story and you, as the speaker, become the narrator or storyteller. Done right, you will take your audience down a magical journey leading down the path, which is your story, holding their attention all the way to the end, to your call to action.

Your Introduction

Your introduction is the most important part of your presentation. If you are not introduced properly by someone else, it is your job to it. Include: Who you are; your name; your company; your background; Why you are there. You are an expert in something, so you have been chosen to speak to this audience. Let them know why you are standing in front of them. What your qualifications are and any other relevant support to help them understand why you are qualified to give this presentation. Tell them the objective of your presentation and what benefits they will gain from participating as an audience member. At this point, they now know why you are there, why they are there and what they plan to get out of it. To be courteous, tell them how long you will be speaking, and you will be taking questions at the end. You might say that you will be speaking for 45 minutes and there will be 15 minutes at the end for questions. Finally, in your introduction include if you will be providing any leave behinds, as in notes, slide summaries or links where they can download additional information.

This type of introduction lets the audience know what to expect, what your position is and what you expect them to do as a result of your presentation. Do you want your audience to approve your recommendations, take action, buy something from you, cancel a previous proposal, or change a strategic direction? Action items may be to write to your congressman, make a financial contribution, approve your proposal, or do your part to help fight crime.

Be specific about what action you want the audience to take. Remember the SMART Acronym. Your action items should be Specific, Measurable, Achievable/Attainable, Relevant and Time-bound. For example, rather than telling an audience that the company needs to reduced expenses, tell them to cut operating costs by 5% by the end of next quarter. Set them straight with their marching orders. Without using SMART your audience either won't know what to do and how they can measure their success. Without a clearly defined set of targets to be able to determine success, there is little chance they will find success.

Sometimes your action item may be more subtle. It may be that you are simply looking for general acceptance of your business strategy or division plans. How do you get that buy in? Ask for it! If your action item requires them to go back and get approval from their management, tell them so. Then set a time for them to get back to you.

Your introduction is the résumé of your presentation skills -- your credibility, your ability to raise and maintain interest, your preparedness and knowledge of the subject matter. Your level of commitment from your audience will be established in the first few minutes of your introduction beginning with your opening statement. In some instances, you have only a few seconds to connect with the audience before you lose them, so an opening statement is critical.

How to Avoid Bragging

Bragging is a sure-fire way to turn a friendly audience into a "So what" or "Who cares" audience. But if you are there to tell them how to be successful or how you accomplished something, how do you do it? To avoid turning off your audience when talking about your accomplishments, start with the challenges you faced and then present a roadmap on how you overcame those challenges. If you start with your challenge, you have a better chance of connecting with the audience and creating that "Tell me more" response. They will want to hear how you got out of that one. It is even better if you can include some errors and missteps you made along the way. If you elaborate on your errors and failures, you have a better chance of your audience connecting with you and wanting to learn more about how you recovered. Personal turnaround stories and the best at getting your point across.

Your Opening Statement

After you have completed the administrative introduction, it is time for your opening statement. Your opening statement will set the tone for your entire presentation. The audience will be judging you from the very first word that comes out of your mouth. If you get off to a great start, you have a better chance of continuing to do great. If you get off to a bumpy start, it will take some extra effort to get out of the hole you got yourself into.

The purpose of your opening statement is to hook your audience. Wake them up. Make them sit up in their chairs. Challenge them. Impress them. Make them sit up and think "Oh man this is going to be good." Coming up with a great creative introduction usually cannot be done until after you have prepared your entire presentation. That is when it all comes together, all your key points are defined, the transitions are done, and you can identify what the ideal introduction will be. There are several different approaches to using an opening statement. Here are some of my favorites

1. **Emotional** – The best way to connect with your audience is to make an emotional connection with them. You do this by telling a story that they can relate to. This story must be relevant to your topic and be tied to the objective of your presentation. If you are making a presentation to investors about a product your company invented to solve a major crisis, you would start by telling a story about that crisis and what the problem is that you plan to solve. Explain how the people that live there are suffering. Draw them in

by tugging on their heart strings. You want the audience to connect with the issue you are presenting so they will follow you through your presentation to find out how you can solve this horrible problem and what you need the audience to do to help you.

2. **Anecdotal** stories are also good as they support your cause and provide some humor at the same time. If the story is personal to you as the presenter, it humanizes you which connects even more with the audience. If you are speaking about home security systems, you could tell a story about when you first got it and one day forgot to shut off the alarm. Boy, was that a surprise when in 4 minutes the police were at the door. That is embarrassing and humanizing and shows the promptness of the service you may be pitching. Taking a personal story and turning into a back handed product testimonial is clever.

3. **Newsworthy**. One of my favorite introduction tools is incorporating a recent news event with the topic I am speaking about. Typically, on the morning of my presentation I will watch the news and read the Wall Street Journal looking for relevant stories to connect to my topic. If my presentation is out of town, chances are slim that anyone else in the audience has read the paper that morning and I will be teaching them something. If you have a current newsworthy item that you incorporate into your introduction, your audience will think how fresh your content is and will think the rest of your presentation is probably going to be just as good. On the contrary, if you start with some old news, your audience will think that the rest of your presentation is stale too.

4. **Rhetorical Questions** are designed to stimulate the brains of your audience. Some rhetorical questions actually get some of the audience members to respond. What if you asked the audience "If you took any species in the entire world and put them in the state of New Jersey, would you think that species would be endangered and near extinction?" I typically get an answer of "yes" or witness a lot of head nodding when I ask that question. This type of a question should be followed with some more riveting information that leads you to your topic.

5. **Factual**. Interesting facts are a great way to start a presentation. Especially those facts that most people do not know. Consider building on the last rhetorical question. If you were giving a presentation about overpopulation in our cities and the need to

decentralize the urban areas, you might mention. "There are 8 billion people on the planet. New Jersey has 205 billion square feet of land. You could put everyone in the entire world in the state of New Jersey and they each would have 25 square feet." Then you can finish with the statement on how we need to decentralize our overcrowded cities and maybe show them the vast lands that are completely vacant and natural. Find some facts that will make your audience think and get them ready to listen to you.

6. **Humor.** Using good humor is good. But using bad or old humor is bad. Never tell an old joke or any joke if there is a chance anyone in the audience ever heard it before. Just like old news will make your presentation appear stale, so will an old joke. Humor should be incorporated throughout your presentation, and it must be relevant to your topic. Self-deprecating humor is always a winner. Making fun of yourself will humanize you and make your audience like you more. Note: Avoid embarrassing personal stories. Self-deprecation humor is one thing but a story that crosses the line is not acceptable. You don't want tell people about an experience you had at a 30-day drug and alcohol rehabilitation center no matter what the point is that you are trying to make. If you are unsure of what is over the line, collaborate with a friend or colleague.

You should tell them after you have piqued their curiosity and have them on the edge of their seat with a thought-provoking opening. If you have used a good introduction, they will eagerly be listening to the details of the agenda to find out what else to expect.

Begin leading your audience to your main topic immediately in your opening statement. Think about it in a way that causes the audience to respond with "Tell me more." If they are interested in the first thing you say, you will subconsciously elicit the "Tell me more" response. Remember, the alternative is the "So what" or "Who Cares" responses, which you definitely want to avoid in your audience. If you open with a current event or interesting fact relevant the audience will think "Tell me more." Describe the event in some, but not excessive detail, then tie it in to your presentation topic. This helps establish credibility with your audience. They will view your information as relevant and up-to-date and will not perceive your talk as just another "canned" presentation.

Some of the best introductions start off with a story or event that appears to be far from the presentation topic. The audience will begin working to figure out how it relates to the topic. As a speaker, you can often see people listening intently, with a furrowed brow, trying to make the connection. This "Tell me more" response is what you want -- the audience is immediately using their brains, getting those wheels in motion. When you make the connection, you have them ready to actively listen to what you say. Sometimes you will even notice slight nods or other signs that they accept your analogy as you tie it all together. Some may even make the connection before you get there. This is great. You have their attention.

Here is an example of a relevant opener I used a few years ago that was far removed from the presentation topic. The audience was a group of field sales agents. The topic is customer-driven marketing and product development. The action item for the audience to join a sales rep product development committee. I began:

> "The cold war between the United States and the Soviet Union was fought on the basis of military superiority. One superpower trying to stockpile their weapons versus another trying to outdo them or develop more sophisticated weapons. Yet, in retrospect, the war was won on the basis of the economy. The free market economy, the one where the customer determines what goods and services are needed and provided in the market, and at what price, won out over an economy where the government determines what is best for the people and what will be sold in the market, and for what price. A centralist body, isolated from its people cannot determine what their customers' needs are.
>
> In the same line, a company cannot sit enclosed within its four walls and make decisions about what our customers need. We need the input of field representatives like you to make sure that our products are meeting our customers' needs. You are out there on the battle lines, in direct contact with customers daily. You know what makes them tick, what piques their interest. That's why we want you to get involved in what we are doing at the corporate home office. That's why we are establishing a sales reps product development committee. Here's how it works and what you can do to take part."

When you are introducing a product, you need to start with some interesting fact that the audience can possibly say "wow, tell me more." Here is an example I did for promoting a software app for managing shared expenses for children of a divorce.

> "Each year there are over 850,000 divorces in this country and 40% of them involve school age children that will continue to have both parents sharing in their care. At the outset it sounds easy, one parent incurs a medical bill of $100 of the child and other parent owes their share. But it is not easy because depending on the type of expense (e.g., medical, day care, college, etc.) the sharing percentages are different. To make it more complicated, some types have deductible like thresholds that must be met before the sharing percentages apply. Just one child can generate over 100 items in a year that need to be shared, and few people have the time or ability to copy the bills, create a spreadsheet and keep it updated. Today we are going to review this product that streamlines and simplifies this process."

Use of Humor

Many presenters try to "break the ice" with the audience by telling an opening joke. But if the purpose to the opening is to stimulate interest in your topic and impart your credibility as an expert in your topic, the use of humor/joke becomes a difficult medium.

For a joke to accomplish all that is required in an introduction, it must be relevant, tied to current events or developments in your topic, and something the audience never heard before. This is a difficult challenge. Just about the worst thing you can do is start off with an inappropriate or stale joke. The audience will think that since the joke is off-target or outdated, the material content of the presentation will probably be the same. You've dug yourself a very deep hole by damaging your credibility. It will be a long uphill struggle just to recover the lost ground.

Don't get me wrong, an opening joke can be effective if related to your topic, current -- and funny. It is the old or ineffective joke that can be disastrous.

Humor though, throughout your presentation, is very effective at keeping your audience engaged and interested. Nothing is better than when your audience laughs and learns at the same time. When they are having a good time, they will surely think "Tell me more." Unfortunately, humor is a very personal thing and how you incorporate humor into your presentation depends on your own personal preferences, your own sense of humor and your ability to use your wit to place humor at the right places in your presentation. Using too much humor or misplaced humor can be counterproductive. However, here are some pointers to use when considering how to incorporate humor

- **Sales Training** – If you are speaking about how to sell any product, avoid using a generic product term (e.g., widget). Make it fun and use a product that you can continue to build your humor on throughout your presentation. For example, if you use "diapers" as a product, you can have many humorous ideas that flow throughout your presentation about diapers like, "Think about cross-selling additional products and services, mention clean up, disinfectant, disposal services, then there is the EPA impact and field study services." There are endless puns that you can flush out with diapers. Sorry, I could not resist.

- **Motivational Speakers** – Humor is essential in motivational speeches. It gets people connected with the speaker and interactivity is important in a motivational setting. Use self-deprecating humor in motivational speeches. Self-deprecating humor is making fun of yourself. It makes people laugh and gets your point across. For some reason, people love to hear stories about how screwed up your life was, how miserable you were and then how you were able to pull it all together and become a success. If you can make them, feel like you had it worse than they do, then they will feel they can make it too.

- **Plea for a cause** – When you ask for money or expecting some specific action, incorporate some humor in your presentation. For example, if you want people to adopt a pet, you might start showing some pictures of some lonely dogs, then jump to a video showing a dog licking its new owner, and then say something like "and all the licks and love comes with no extra charge."

- **Financial Presentations** – Generally, humor in financial presentations is extremely difficult and, depending upon the audience, should probably be avoided.

The Main Content

Once you have completed your opening, lead right into the meat of your presentation where you make your key points that support your objective and your message. Introduce your proposed plan of action, solution, or opinion. This lays the groundwork for the rest of your presentation.

The most important part of an effective presentation is a clear singular theme. FACT: Over time, most members of the audience will only remember one message from your presentation. Rarely will someone be able to list multiple points that a presenter made. For example, from a financial presentation about the success of the company, one would likely remember that the company is doing well compared with plan, but few will remember the individual indicators and the related reasons for such success.

Identifying a singular theme can be difficult for many speakers. But when they do, preparation of the presentation becomes easier, and the presentation rises to a whole new level. Ask most speakers for the one point they want the audience to walk away with, and the response is commonly "I have several points." But, remembering that the audience will likely remember one thing only, you must identify the common thread to all your points and focus on it. Once you identify your theme, make sure everything you say reinforces that point.

For example: A presentation for an education materials company was being made by the home office to its sales force. Before the presentation was made, the speaker indicated that there were six main topics each with multiple points of detail. One topic was a new education program; another was an expanded program updated from the previous version; another was a completely rewritten program. (I cannot even remember the other three topics). The speaker was noticeably confident that the audience would remember all of the points for the different programs and was convinced that there were multiple points to the presentation.

After listening to the entire presentation at a rehearsal, we were able to identify the common thread: "The Company's education materials and programs are kept current with frequent updates to enhance them to meet the ever-changing needs of our clients." Were the salespeople interested in knowing the details of the enhancements of each program? No, they wanted something they could sell. With the identification of this single theme, the speaker was able to develop an introduction that was strong and effective, and then reinforce the main theme throughout the presentation. The salespeople in the audience got what they wanted, a selling edge over the competition. While touting their materials over those of their competitors (which were stale and not in sync with the business needs of the customers), they now have a very real selling point to take home from the presentation. They were not forced to weed through six messages with multiple sub plots.

Your Key Points

You should strive to have between 3 to 5 key supporting points as this is manageable for you and your audience. Any more will get confusing, making it difficult to keep track, and any less will make it seem like you do not have enough to substantiate your claim. Each key point is typically its own slide heading. The bullets on the slide elaborate to support this point.

Keep the information concise and relevant to your topic. Too much information will obscure the message. If you are selling products or services avoid talking about features. Features are a list of characteristics of a product or service that requires the listener to work too hard to figure what the feature is, what problems it could solve and if it would apply in their world. It's better to talk benefits and results to avoid the audiences' brains working overtime.

There are a few ways to organize your information to support your key points. But the approach that makes the most sense is to start with a strong solid statement, then proceed to provide the details to back it up, whether that is charts, graphs, tables, statements, or images, and walk them through the details. Find verifiable information to substantiate and support your points. Make sure your support is clear as to how it supports your point. Anything that is ambiguous and subject to multiple interpretations, should be left out. These can be facts or anecdotes, customer testimonials, independent lab certifications or other references. When considering the support for your claims, decide how you want to present the information. Will you tell a story, show a chart or graph, present an image or picture or just simply state it? If you cannot support a key point, you should not include it. You do not want to damage your credibility by posting something that supports your point, but it is not true or is misleading. Remember, everything on the internet is not always accurate.

After you make your key point and provide support it is time to summarize how it reinforces the point and the main theme and then transition to the next key point. Smooth transitions make you look very professional.

Your Closing

After you have covered all your key points that support your main theme and provided adequate support, it is time to transition to your closing. First and foremost, it is important to restate your main theme, to remind them why you are there. Briefly tie your key points together as to how they support your objective. You cannot enter any new information at this point in the presentation. New information belongs in the body, not when you are closing. Incorporate some inspirational tidbits of knowledge or information. You want to make a memorable impression on your audience so this is a chance to reach out and connect with them again. Thank the audience for their time and consideration. And then hit them with your call to action. What is it that you want them to do as a result of your presentation? State it directly. Tell them exactly what you want to do.

Remember to make it SMART, Specific, Measurable, Achievable/Attainable, Relevant and Time-bound. You may want them to buy your product within a certain period to obtain the offered discount.

You may want them to go to a link on the internet and purchase your product or service. These are specific and measurable, and we can see it is relevant to your presentation and you gave them a time limit.

But is it achievable? Often that is the one thing that is the stumbling block. Do they know where to buy your product? Do they have the online link to complete the transaction? Do they need to be on their computer to do it or can they do it from their smart phones? I recall working with one company where their call to action was to go to their website from their home computers and sign up for a service, which cost $150 per year.

They made their presentations to groups of about 100 all over the country and they handed out cards with the URL link on it to complete the online purchase transaction. They were getting about 10% signed up. "Attainable" was the problem. I worked with them to change the process to make the form accessible from their smart phones. At the end of the presentation, they walked everyone through the process of signing up on their phone as part of the closing. In the very first presentation they got 70 sign ups when they changed to this method. That is 70% versus 10% or $10,500 versus $1,500, just in one presentation. Make it easy for them to complete your call to action and they will.

Address your Target Audience

"Designing a presentation without an audience in mind is like writing a love letter and addressing it: To Whom It May Concern." – Ken Haemer

A stellar presentation to one audience may be a disastrous presentation to another. That is why the presentation must be tailored to the specific needs of the audience.

Let's assume that you are giving a presentation on how the company uses R&D to remain the industry leader in technology, earn a reasonable profit and remain competitively priced. The different audiences for your presentation include the following:

- Board of Directors and shareholders
- Senior management
- The sales force
- Customers and potential customers
- Production workers

Each group has a different need to be fulfilled. Shareholders want a good return on their investment. The sales force wants competitive products and a flexible pricing structure to allow them to sell effectively.

Customers want quality at an appropriate price. Production workers want good working conditions and a decent salary. Senior management needs to balance the needs of all these groups.

It would be impossible to give the exact same R&D presentation to the sales force, customers, employees and shareholders. If you focus on competitive prices, your customers will love you, but shareholders will think you are not applying your working capital properly and giving away their profits. On the other hand, if you focus on profit margins, shareholders will be happy, but your customers will think that prices are too high, and employees may think their salaries are too low.

Make sure your primary point is in line with your audience. The only presentation that is suited for all audiences is one that is so general that it is not very informative.

WIIFM – What's In It For Me?

People act for one of two reasons, fear and love. Many decisions are made because people fear the consequences of not acting on certain things. Or because they love the feeling or the outcome that the results bring. Your goal is to figure out what your audience will act on – what they fear and/or love – and connect your calls to action accordingly. In business, your audience may be fearful of losing their job and not be able to pay their bills, so they may be intune with your presentation if it helps them keep their jobs. They may love the feeling of giving to a charity, so your call to action may tug on those heart strings. There was a Seinfeld episode with the premise that everyone does everything for either fear or love, and they tried to disprove that premise throughout the episode. There were not able to.

When crafting your presentation and your calls to action, keep in mind WIIFM, because if they don't feel they are getting anything out of your requested calls to action, they probably won't be inclined to act.

Rhetorically Create an Awareness in Your Audience

"Tell me and I forget. Teach me and I remember. Involve me and I learn." – Benjamin Franklin

Audiences like to feel a part of the presentation. A good thought-provoking introduction is one way to get them involved. Another is to incorporate rhetorical questions into your presentations -- questions that you are not expecting the audience to answer, but that you use to make the audience think along with you. Statement, after statement, after statement can lull your audience to sleep. But incorporating rhetorical questions makes a connection with the audience and keeps them involved. It stimulates the brain and draws them into a dialog about the question being presented, even though there is no actual dialog.

Some examples of rhetorical questions that can be effective are as follows:

- If we keep doing the same thing over and over, are we to expect different results?
- If practice makes perfect, but nobody is perfect, then why practice?

When using rhetorical questions remember to make your questions easy to follow and easy to answer by keeping your questions short and concise. Consider asking a few questions in a row to keep their brains working and building up their interest. When asking questions, pick one or two people in the audience and maintain eye contact with them through the entire question. Address the question to them directly and they will feel compelled to answer the question, even though you are not looking for an answer. Also, do not just use these questions in the beginning, sprinkle them throughout your presentation.

6. PRESENTATION DELIVERY

"The most important thing in communication is to hear what is not being said." -- Peter F. Drucker

Just as important as what you say is how you say it. This section is devoted to improving the "how" -- presentation delivery. In a later chapter we will address the "what" -- presentation content.

Delivery is a catch-all category for everything other than content, and it takes on many forms. Delivery includes voice tone and inflection, dress, posture, hair style, organization, hand-outs, visual aids, timeliness, breathing, speed, attitude, movement, eye contact -- even the way you shuffle your notes. Let's examine a few of these elements of delivery.

Use an Agenda with Associated Times Listed

Treat your audience like V.I.P.s -- people who have things to do and places to go. They have likely juggled their schedules to attend your presentation and allotted a specific amount of time in their busy day. If your presentation is one in a series of presentations in a day-long meeting, many attendees will be conducting business during the breaks and lunch. They need to know what to expect regarding their schedules. They need to know how much time is allotted to each and every segment of the presentation.

This is important to you for two reasons. First, the audience will be monitoring the progress of each segment against the timeline, to see if the agenda is ahead or behind schedule, so they can adjust their schedules accordingly. For example, when the audience checks back in with the office to conduct business, they might say, "We are 25 minutes behind schedule and are scheduled for a break at 3:15, so plan on me checking back in at about 3:40."

Second, certain members of the audience may opt to skip certain presentations they feel are not important to them. Knowing exactly when the following segment will begin allows them to gauge their return to the session.

Times should be assigned to each segment of an entire day's agenda. Likewise, for long sessions you should try to assign times to each segment of your presentation. The audience would like to see the outline of what you are going to cover and how long you will be spending on each topic. This establishes credibility by demonstrating that you thoughtfully planned out your presentation and were sensitive to the audience's needs. Without a detailed agenda with times assigned, the audience may begin wondering where you are headed and whether you are on track with your time allotment.

If you are organizing an entire agenda with multiple speakers, include the names and titles of each speaker for the presentation segments. If a speaker will appear more than once on your agenda, only the name needs to be listed the subsequent times. When appropriate, include a biography or short statement that addresses the specialties and background of each speaker.

Sample agenda for an entire day of presentations:

ABC Company

General Description of Meeting - Location

October 19, 20XX 9:00 a.m. - 5:00 p.m.

8:30 - 9:00	Registration	
9:00 - 9:10	Administration and Logistics	Thomas White, VP of Marketing
9:10 - 9:30	Introduction and Overview of Agenda	Thomas White
9:30 - 9:45	ABC Company - Company Overview and future direction	Bill Black, President
9:45 - 10:15	ABC Company - Financial results to date and plan for the 20XX	Bob Redding, Controller
10:15 - 10:30	COFFEE BREAK	
10:30 - 11:30	Product Development	Joni Brown, VP Product Development
11:30 - 12:00	Breakout Group Topic Assignments	Thomas White
12:00 - 1:00	LUNCH	
1:00 - 2:00	Breakout Group sessions	
2:00 - 2:45	Marketing & Advertising	Pat Green, VP Mktg
2:45 - 3:15	Reports from Breakout groups	
3:15 - 3:30	BREAK	
3:30 - 4:30	Reports from Breakout groups (Cont.)	
4:30 - 5:00	Wrap up and open discussion	Thomas White

<u>Sample agenda for one presentation within a larger agenda</u>

ABC Company

Financial Results to Date and Plan for 20XX

Bob Redding, Controller

October 19, 20XX

9:45 a.m. - 10:15 a.m.

Introduction	5 Minutes
Review of 6 months' Financial Statements	10 minutes
Explanation of Variances	5 minutes
Outlook for remainder of 20XX	5 minutes
Questions	5 minutes

Notice that the overview agenda has clock times, and the detailed agenda has minutes for each section. This is recommended because agendas can get jumbled or delayed. Still, an estimated beginning and ending time will give the clock watchers a target to shoot for. In essence, this is "synchronizing your watch" with your audience.

Finish Early

Few speakers ever finished a presentation early with the audience wishing that it would go on for another 20 minutes. It is prudent, therefore, to overestimate the length of your presentation and, if anything, surprise your audience with an early finish. Too many speakers underestimate the amount of material they have and go over their time allotment.

If your material runs long or results in more questions than anticipated, you will need to cut short your presentation or cut off the questions. It is discourteous to your audience and to other speakers to go over time. If you tell them you will wrap it up by 5:00 p.m. you need to finish on time.

If you are last in a series of speakers and you are introduced at or near the announced ending time of the agenda, you have a problem. The reason that you are starting late may be the culmination of several speakers before you going overtime only 5 minutes, but that is academic now. Do you complete your full-length presentation knowing that the audience may have other engagements? Do you do an abbreviated version, cutting yourself and your audience short? Or do you reschedule your presentation for those who have to leave? There is no absolute answer. Each case needs to be looked at independently -- and the audience must be the ones to decide.

If this happens to you, identify the time issue immediately before you begin. For example, you might say:

"I was scheduled to begin at 4:30 p.m. and had planned on a twenty-minute presentation, allowing for ten minutes of questions. But looking at the big clock on the wall, we see that it is already 5:15 p.m. I really need the full twenty minutes and do not want to shortchange you. I understand that some people have to go, and I would be glad to reschedule early next week with a smaller group if you would like. Just leave your business card with me and we will set it up. For those of you that can stay, great! We will proceed. I will not disappoint you."

By identifying the problem upfront, you are demonstrating that you can relate to the audience and understand its needs. You have presented those who really must leave the opportunity to see you later the next week. Others who are really interested will stay the overtime to hear you speak. The mere fact that you offered to go out of your way for the audience will make them want to stay. Now you are ready to proceed with your presentation.

The worst experience I had with this was as an audience member attending a full day event. The list of speakers was very impressive, which was why I wanted to attend. The conference fee offered an option for an additional $200 be one of 20 audience members to have a private lunch with the speakers and that included a separate happy hour at 5 pm. By lunchtime, they were running 1.5 hours behind schedule, so to make up time, they had the lunch brought in and we ate at the tables while they tried to catch up on the agenda. So much for that private lunch with the speakers. I found the meeting facilitator and asked about the agenda and timing being way off, and his response was "Isn't this great! These speakers have so much to say. We are really getting our money's worth." I was stunned by his response. I asked him what about the private lunch with the speakers and he told me they will make up for it later. As the clock approached 5 pm, the scheduled happy hour time, another speaker took to the stage. I was confused since the previous speaker was the one listed last on the agenda. They explained that he had to catch a flight so they moved him up on the agenda so he could leave on time. This clearly left the entire audience without any idea of how many speakers were left and when this day would be over. They actually had 3 more speakers. By 7 pm more than half the audience had left, most of the speakers left to catch flights home and others were still speaking. There was no private lunch or private happy hour with the speakers and the perception of the event was a total disaster.

If they kept to the agenda, it would have been a success. The following year I got an invitation to attend the second annual event. They ultimately had to cancel it because no one signed up because of the organization's failures the first year.

If you are a facilitator of the event, you must take charge of your speakers. Most of the speakers love to hear themselves talk and will gladly go over time if you let them. Also, some speakers may be frequent speakers that have canned presentations of a certain length, and they may not adjust it to your allotted time schedule. Have someone in the back of the room hold up signs for 10 minutes, 5 minutes, 2 minutes, 1 minute and 0 minutes. The speaker can see them and adjust his talk accordingly. A speaker will not look at the clock and figure out when they should wrap up, but when an actual person is telling them with these signs to wrap up, they will comply. It's very subtle pressure, but pressure enough to keep on track. The best events I have ever been to are those that religiously keep to their listed time schedules.

Suggested content to keep the presentation focused

Sample Agendas for various topics

Recommending a Strategy

1. Vision Statement
   - Vision and long-term direction
   - Goal and objective
2. Today's Situation
   - Summary of the current situation
   - How did we get here?
   - Relevant historical information
   - Original assumptions that are no longer valid
3. Available Options
   - Alternate strategies
   - Advantages & disadvantages of each
   - Cost of each option
4. Recommendation
   - Recommended strategies
   - Projected results
5. What to do next
   - Action items for audience

Training

1. Introduction
   - Define subject matter
   - State what audience will learn
   - Find out relevant background and interest of audience
2. Agenda
   - List topics to be covered
   - List times allotted to each
3. Overview
   - Give big picture of subject
   - Explain how individual topics fit together
   - Define terms as used
4. For each topic
   - Explain details
   - Give example
   - Hands-on exercise to reinforce learning
5. Summary
   - State what has been learned
   - Define ways to apply training
   - Request feedback of training session
   - Identify where to get more information
   - Recommend other training sessions
   - List books, articles, electronic sources
   - Identify consulting services, other sources

Communicating Bad News

1. Current Situation
   - State the bad news, clearly, fully
   - Explain how it happened?
   - Provide relevant history, facts, strategies
   - Dispel invalid assumptions
2. Alternatives Considered
   - Present alternate courses of action
   - Discuss pros/cons of each
3. Recommendation or Decision
   - State recommended course of action or decision
   - Discuss how recommendation addresses problem
   - Discuss how plan addresses hardships resulting from action
4. Vision for the Future
   - Reaffirm goals
   - Set expectations for future
   - Set time for expected results
5. Summary
   - Summarize key points that give audience confidence and improve morale

Selling an Idea or a Product

1. Objective
   - State the desired objective product or idea will satisfy
   - Use multiple points if necessary
2. Customer Requirements
   - State the needs of the audience
   - Identify additional audience needs perceived
3. Meeting Needs
   - List products and features
   - Explain how each addresses specific need or solves specific problem
4. Cost Analysis
   - Point out financial benefits to customer
   - Compare cost-benefits between you and competitors
5. Summary
   - Repeat key benefits provided by the product, service, or idea being promoted

Reporting Status or Progress

1. Define subject
    - List main subject components
    - Report overall status
2. Project Status
    - Present schedule or timeline
    - Describe team involved
    - Describe scope or goals
    - Describe to-date accomplishments
    - Elaborate on current issues
    - Explain what was learned during period of report
3. Key Issues
    - Prioritize issues
    - Suggest courses of action
4. Next Steps
    - Summarize past actions taken
    - Specify future actions
    - Define requirements you have of your audience
    - Suggest a time and place for the next status report

General

1. Introduction
    - State purpose of discussion
    - Identify yourself
    - Present topics of discussion
    - State main ideas you'll address
2. Each topic
    - Give details about topic
    - Supply supporting information and example
    - Explain how topic relates to your audience
3. Summarize Key Points
4. Next Steps
    - Outline actions required of audience
    - Summarize follow-up actions required of you

Eye-Contact

"The eyes are the windows to your soul." – William Shakespeare

If the eyes are the window to the soul, then you cannot fully understand what someone is saying unless you can look straight into their eyes. This is true whether you are carrying on a conversation with a single individual or are in front of a group of 200+ people. In order to "see" what the other person is saying, you need to establish eye contact. Eye contact also raises the attention level of the people you connect with.

How do you make eye contact with a large audience? The answer is simple, "One person at a time!"

As you speak, move your eyes about the room, establishing and maintaining eye-contact with different individuals. Select your "contacts" on the basis of their location in the audience. One effective technique is to divide the room up into four sections. Establish contact with one person from a section and then move to another person in the second section, then the third, then the fourth. Do not return to the first section until you have established eye-contact with one person from all the other sections. If on the other hand, you focus exclusively on one section of the audience, the other sections of the room will think you forgot them and may begin their own conversations.

It is most effective to maintain eye contact with each individual for 3-6 seconds. More than six seconds, the individual might become intimidated; any less than three seconds is not enough time to establish an "eye-to-eye" relationship.

One common mistake made by presenters is to look above the heads of the audience. This fails to establish a relationship with the audience and, worse the audience will be distracted wondering what or who you are looking at. If the audience does not feel that you are addressing them and their specific needs, they will not feel the need to pay attention.

Besides establishing a relationship with the audience, maintaining eye contact facilitates your ability to keep on track. When you are looking someone right in the eye as you are making your point, you remain focused. It is like carrying on a conversation with one person in private. On the other hand, if you are glancing around the room avoiding one-to-one eye contact, you have more of a tendency to lose focus forgetting where you are, the exact point you were going to make, or where your point was headed.

Speak Loudly From Your Diaphragm

Speaking loudly not only allows your audience to hear you, it projects your confidence. Most people will need to practice speaking loud enough for a large audience to hear them. Speaking should not be a by-product of breathing. It needs to be the driving force behind the breathing.

Speaking loudly comes from speaking from the diaphragm, a muscle above the stomach that pushes air out of the lungs. Speaking loudly and confidently requires forming words and forcing air out from the diaphragm. Standing allows the diaphragm to move freely and naturally. While sitting, the diaphragm may be restricted. If you have to sit while speaking, sit up straight, no slouching, and this will allow you diaphragm to be able to work without being hindered.

Three Speaking Styles to Avoid

There are three styles of speech that commonly sabotage a presentation:

1. **The trailing sentence.**

   The trailing sentence occurs when the speaker takes a deep breath and exhales as the sentence is spoken. The first words of the sentence receive the greatest emphasis, then the volume continually decreases as the air runs out. Each and every sentence starts out strong and trails off, both in emphasis and volume, until the audience can barely hear the end of the sentence.

   Under this style of speaking, the words that should be stressed and emphasized are not, unless, or course, they happen to be at the beginning of the sentence. For an effective presentation, the important words need to be stressed wherever they appear in the sentence.

2. **Thinking ahead to the next sentence**

   This style is evidenced by a speaker pausing in the middle of a sentence when a pause is not justified or planned. Often, the speaker is also adjusting his notes, organizing the next slide or fiddling with the overhead. It is obvious that the person is preparing for the next thought before finishing the previous one.

   To avoid this distractive style, be sure to complete your thoughts and sentences. If there is some preparation to be done to shift gears to the next topic, pause between topics. The pause may seem like an eternity to you but is much less distracting to the audience than pausing midstream.

3. **The roller coaster ride**

   The roller coaster ride may be another by-product of thinking ahead. This style is evident when the speaker is talking fast and for no apparent reason and then slows down. Then, also for no apparent reason, they speed up again. Often the speaker is talking quickly or at normal speed while looking at the audience. Then, when looking down at their notes, the speed slows, as if they are planning the next point to make. Speakers should try to develop a comfortable and consistent delivery speed and vary from it only to add emphasis.

Ramble Check

During your presentation, periodically ask yourself, "Is what I am saying supporting my main point? Or am I off on a tangent that the audience may not care about?" "Am I still taking my audience on a magical journey?" "Are they still in that "Tell me more" state or have I lost them?" "Have they have shifted into the "Who cares" state of mind and cannot wait for it to be over?"

Some people seem to like the sound of their own voices. No matter how much they lay out the structure of their presentation and the related times for each section, they always seem to take off on an irrelevant tangent. Invariably these speakers run over their allotted time. When asked why they went overtime, they will inevitably respond that the audience was so interested in what they had to say, it forced them to go over. How untrue! The audience likes to stay focused on the main point and so should you. So, check yourself often.

Show Your Passion and Enthusiasm

"By inflection you can say much more than your words do." –
Malcolm S. Forbes

When two people carry a one-on-one conversation on a topic that interests them, both parties talk with emotion and enthusiasm. They are animated and dynamic. They wave their arms, sigh, shake their heads, and use inflection in their voice. Without hearing them, you can tell they are really involved in what they are talking about.

That same level of enthusiasm and energy can be carried over to your presentations. Your audience will thank you for it. The more you can demonstrate your enthusiasm and excitement in your topic, the more the audience will be excited and interested in what you have to say. If you demonstrate passion about your topic, they will get themselves geared up for a high-energy presentation.

Focus on conveying enthusiasm and passion. Do not be afraid to use a variety of tones and inflections in your voice. It is a lot more effective to demonstrate your excitement than to stand motionless and emotionless speaking in a monotone voice.

Financial presentations may seem to be the most difficult to get excited about. But there is nothing more exciting to executives than meeting or exceeded an aggressive business goal; or more compelling than dealing with changing market conditions that resulted in you not meeting your goals. The passion comes in your ability to explain what happened and describe how you will address the future based upon what happened in the past.

Incorporating enthusiasm into any presentation increases the attention level of your audience -- and is a lot more fun for the speaker. And fun is better!

Attitude - Look Forward to the Presentation

A speaker in waiting will sometimes think or even utter, "I can't wait until it is over!" "It," being the presentation. Is this the sound of a confident individual? No. Someone who is thoroughly prepared, organized, practiced, and confident should look forward to the event, not dread it.

Attitude is so important. If you are looking forward to the completion of the presentation, the audience can sense it. You rush through areas that require more time. You cut off some of the required emphasis and passion in order to get completed faster. These hurry-up tactics all have negative effects on your presentation. You may feel good when you are done, but you have just short-changed your credibility and your audience.

To improve attitude, a speaker needs to be his or her own cheerleader, providing kudos at every turn. You should have benchmarks within your presentation and if you hit them, put a check in your column. Check marks could be given for adding extra emphasis at certain points, taking your time during certain sections, reeling in the audience with your thought-provoking introduction, hitting certain time check points, or getting a desired response from your audience. Keep a mental scorecard in your head. The presentation then becomes a challenging game. You versus yourself. What you planned versus what happens. Later, you can "score" your success on an overall basis.

This is the best type of game. You control how the scoring is done, you are responsible for recording the score, and you are your own toughest judge of success. When you look at a presentation as a game, one you look forward to winning, your attitude toward the presentation changes. No longer do you dread your mission; you get psyched up for it. You still have nervous butterflies in your stomach, but that is all part of the excitement of the game.

Should You Read Your Presentation?

There are three different ways to deliver a presentation: reading from a script or teleprompter, using bullets on note cards, or memorization. Perhaps the most boring and painful thing in the business world is listening to someone read a prepared speech written down on paper. Often, the speaker is hidden behind a podium, embracing it like a shield, and keeping his or her head down looking at his or her notes to avoid looking into the eyes of the audience.

The problems with this style of presentation are monumental. First, when a speaker is reading prepared text, there is no connection between audience and speaker. The speaker is in his own little world of reading and largely unaware of the audience. And the audience, whether a small group of ten, or a large group of a hundred or even a thousand, can sense this. Some of them may wonder "Who is the speaker is talking to?"

Being read to is boring. The speaker is merely reciting words on a page. The message is not coming from the heart. This may be fine when politicians read from a teleprompter to make sure they hit the exact points in the exact manner they intended, but when businesspeople read from scripts or a teleprompter, it often falls flat, and the audience disengages.

The second method is using outline notes or note cards and speaking from the heart which is so much more interesting. In order to really connect with the audience, it must come from the heart and if you are telling a story they will enjoy participating in the magical journey of your presentation.

When presenting something highly technical, you can read a limited amount of text to assure your audience that you got it right. But the rest of the presentation should be from notes and from within. If you do have to read, explain that to the audience. Tell them that because you want to get it verbatim, bear with you while the statement is read.

When you maintain eye contact as you talk, you can often sense what points the audience are most interested in. Once you identify a special interest, you can apply more emphasis. If you are reading a prepared text, however, you will not be able to read the audience. You won't identify the audience's special interest and you will not be able to make adjustments. Reading is also inflexible when you need to handle audience questions that you planned to address later on in your prepared text. If you answer them now, what do you do when you get to the prepared text later? Repeat yourself? You might as well, since the audience may be asleep by then anyway and not remember it is something they already heard.

Memorization Is Best, If You Have the Time

If reading is not allowed, is memorizing the text the way to go? Verbatim memorization of a presentation is extremely difficult and takes a lot of practice. However, if you are making a presentation that has be exact, and a team of people worked on the script to get the right words in the right spot of the presentation, you must memorize it to get the desired effect. For example, if you are making a presentation to some potential investors you want to make sure that you use the exact words that will maximize the results. You must memorize not only the text but the passion, the points of emphasis, your movements, your facial expressions, and attitude. Otherwise, you do not come across as genuine. It is possible but it takes a lot of practice.

When you are telling a story, it is easier to memorize your speech because you are going on that magical journey with your audience and one sentence should naturally follow the last. But it is still not easy to memorize a long speech entirely.

If you do memorize it, it will probably be apparent to your audience. You'll be so wrapped up in remembering the exact words that your focus is not on the audience, but rather the next line that you memorized. The situation becomes worse if you lose your place and become stuck trying to remember where you left off. This can be awkward, and the audience may cringe feeling for you. At least a reader has the text to help get back on track.

Remember to maintain eye contact and establish a connection with your audience. Two things that cannot be accomplished using reading or memorization. When you are taking them on your magical journey reading and memorization is a guaranteed way the audience may not be going on that journey with you unless you can adequately show passion and enthusiasm.

Say It Straight - Don't Make Your Audience Work

Many speakers try to make the idea or concept they are attempting to convey more impressive or complex than it needs to be. Keep your message simple, so the audience does not have to work to figure it out. Give your audience credit. They are intelligent and can figure out what you are talking about, unless you confuse them. If your audience does not "get it," they will probably ask interruptive questions or give up and ignore the rest of your presentation.

The proper way to speak is to make your statement first, then follow it up with supporting facts that you based your conclusion. Many speakers start off with a bunch of facts, one after the other, and finish with the statement. This makes the audience work too hard and you may lose them along the way. If you start off with "I believe we should [SOME STRATEGY OR IDEA]" and then proceed to support it with your reasoning. You have a better chance of keeping your audience engaged than if you start throwing out your rationale first and hope they are still with you by the time you state your position.

In personal one-on-one communication I often see two problems. First, the person lists a bunch of reasons before they state their position. Again, this makes the listener work to try and figure out where they are going. They should state their position first, then provide supporting details. Think about a newspaper. You read the headline, then if you are interested you read the first paragraph to get more information, and if you are still interested you read on.

As an example, a couple is talking, and the wife says something like "The heat in the car did not work too well today." The husband is not sure where she is going with this, so he says, "I'll take it to the mechanic on Monday." She goes on to tell him that the engine is making some funky noise. He responds with "I'll have him look at that too." She continues to mention that the brakes are squealing. All this time the husband has no idea what her real point is. If she just started out saying "Honey, I think we need to get a new car." And then listed the reasons, it would be a much better conversation.

The second personal communication failure is when one person makes a statement that may be controversial and cannot support that statement with reasons why they have that position. I see this is in political discussions frequently. For example, if one person says, "I think this President is horrible." The next question would be "Why?" and generally, there is no logical rationale that supports that statement.

It is always better to start with your statement and back it up with some good solid position statements to support your initial statement, whether it is in your personal communications or in front of a large audience.

Use Questions to Keep the Audience Alert

Ask questions of the audience to mix your presentation up a little. Even rhetorical questions make the audience think. For example, "How can we combat the extreme competitive pressures being applied in the market today?" A dramatic pause with a look around the audience. "Let's take a look at the marketing plan for the next 12 months..."

If the audience is not too large, you can also elicit actual answers from them, but be careful as this often tends to result in presentations that go over your allotted time.

Remember to Breathe and Take a Breather (pause)

Take advantage of commas and periods, as well as your well positioned pauses, for gathering air. If you find yourself running out of breath, relax and take your time. The importance of taking time to breathe cannot be over-stressed.

Look Good (No Distractions)

I was at a three-day seminar where approximately 500 people attended. The structure of the seminar included general sessions for all audiences and small break-out groups for the audience to select and attend. During one of the breaks, this guy came up to me. He asked me a question, which I did not hear. He was loud enough and clear enough for the surrounding setting, but I still could not hear him.

His appearance spoke so loudly that I was completely distracted to the point my ears heard nothing. He had shoulder length hair, most of it in dreadlocks with some of the ends partially spiked and dyed green. He had a goatee, also with the tip dyed green. He had a ring piercing his lip and several in his ears. He was wearing very expensive sneakers, trousers that were too large and an old army jacket that hung down to his knees.

I was so overwhelmed by his appearance that I could not hear anything he said. My senses were busy absorbing the complete picture before me. After asking him twice to repeat himself, I was able to hear what he said on his third try. He wanted a job. It took me that long to absorb and accept his appearance to allow my ears to hear again.

People in a one-on-one conversation tend to have the highest level of attention for each other. But in this example, there was such a large number of distractions, listening was, at first, impossible. If an appearance can be so distracting to a person in a one-on-one conversation, think about what impact it could have on a speaker to an audience.

You do not want your audience distracted or murmuring amongst themselves about some aspect of your appearance. Eliminate distractions so they can focus on you and what you must tell them.

Clothes

Wearing the right clothing will not automatically result in a successful presentation. But appearing in inappropriate attire will make it much more difficult for you to be successful. The rule for clothing is simple: "Dress at least as well as your audience!" If your meeting is professional attire, you should look your best with a nice suit. If your audience is "business casual" you should dress at least upscale business casual, with a suit still a preferable choice. The decision to dress down from a suit should depend upon your relationship with the audience.

Unknown audiences should always be approached in a suit, which serves as a statement of confidence and professionalism, and helps you establish credibility.

Colors

When considering the type of suit to be wearing, remember that loud bright colors are distracting, while soft colors may present you as weak. If you want people to agree with you, "blue" is the tried-and-true way to go. Blue is pleasing and inoffensive, yet powerful. It presents you in a confident manner. The best colors for a speaker are as follows:

- Dark blue
- Medium Blue
- Grey Blue
- Charcoal Gray
- Olive Green
- Black (for women)

The colors may sound pretty boring, but it is not your clothes that you want the audience to focus on. You want them to focus on you and your topic without distracting them by inappropriate or overwhelming attire.

It is difficult to list all of the colors to avoid because situations differ and there are so many colors. As a rule, colors you should stay away from for a suit are:

- Pastels
- Black (for men)
- Red
- Orange
- Other bright colors

Shirts/blouses are best if they are solid light colors like grey or white. Stripes should be avoided unless they are very thin. Thick stripes are distracting and can take attention away from your message.

When using accent colors like ties or scarfs, the concept is a little different. These items should coordinate with your outfit yet should be chosen to go with your mission. If you want to appear powerful, a bright tie, preferably red, is most effective. If you are trying to win someone over to your point of view and do not want to offend them, then a friendly colorful tie will do the trick. Ties with cartoon characters on them should be avoided if you want anyone to take you seriously. Wearing a gray or duller colored tie or scarf, will not provide the necessary accent needed.

When in doubt, go more conservative with the suit and shirt, and go with a colorful but serious tie.

Clothing Style

Styles of clothing can change rapidly, but men's conservative, classic clothing has not changed much at all. The proper accents can make the traditional suit up-to-date. Women should also dress conservatively, depending on the presentation, though. Dress appropriately based on what your objectives are and not to be a distraction. The general style rule is simple: If in doubt, it may be a distraction, don't do it.

Jacket On or Off?

Wearing a jacket in front of a group presents a complete package. It is professional, neat, and organized. Without saying a word, you are starting on the plus side.

After you begin your presentation and establish your credibility, you may take off your jacket if you feel it's appropriate for the audience. In fact, taking off your jacket before conveying an important point can help grab your audience's attention.

Face

Before you start, take a quick check in a mirror to make sure that there is no food in your teeth, your hair is not messed, and your makeup is right. The couple of minutes it takes to make the last-minute check will be invaluable to you if there is some last-minute correction required.

Hair

Hair styles come and go, but generally, as with suits and clothes, a conservative style is best when speaking in front of a group. Wild and crazy hair may be appropriate for special purposes, but generally it is a distraction. Hair styles are more accepting than clothes because they need to be pretty wild to be unacceptable for a presentation. The hair described previously with the individual asking for a job, is an example of an extreme which should be avoided.

Shoes

Stand in front of a group with clean and polished shoes and no one will notice. Stand in front of a group with dirty and dull shoes and your credibility can be tarnished. There is something unique about shoes that cause people to ignore them when they are clean and polished but notice them when they are not.

Stand Tall and Maintain Good Posture

Standing with good posture and your hands at your sides is a powerful position. Your points come across stronger and more confident. Leaning to the side or slouching forward weakens your posture and image dramatically. It may not seem like much, but poor posture conveys inferiority. Still, you want to look natural, not stiff, which is a distraction to your audience as well.

Relaxation is important to looking natural. Your audience will be relaxed if you look relaxed. Relax, but stand tall and maintain good posture.

What To Do With Your Hands

Your hands are your most powerful body language tool but can be awkward appendages when not in use. When not gesturing keep your hands at your sides, right at the ends of your arms where they belong. This looks natural and lends to good posture. Avoid doing the following with your hands:

- Putting them in the fig leave position - clasped together in front of your body. It looks like you are hiding something.
- Putting them behind your back - it makes you look too care-free or too nonchalant to be addressing a serious topic.
- Putting them in your pockets. Again, you look like you are concealing something. Jingling coins or keys is particularly distracting.
- Holding them chest or waist high either together or apart. It just does not look natural, and often makes you resemble a penguin or raptor.

Relax. Your hands look natural just hanging by your sides.

When you are gesturing, use your hands to display your emotion and to get your point across. Use your hands and arms completely. If you are demonstrating that something encompasses the *whole ball of wax*, for example, use your entire wingspan. Throughout your presentation, check the positioning of your hands and ask yourself if they are where they should be.

Working With / Against the Podium

Many speakers feel uncomfortable standing in front of groups without a podium to lean on, hide behind, or rest their notes and visual aids upon. But podiums hide the body, making it more difficult to show your emotion. The audience needs to sense how you really feel about your topic, and they can do this easiest by observing your body language. The soul of your presentation comes from how you act and look. And if you are hiding most of your body behind a podium, the audience may never get the full effect of what you are saying.

A common mistake among nervous speakers is to stand with one foot on the podium step and grasp both sides of the podium -- like hanging onto a cliff. They use their arms and hands to flip the pages of their notes and occasionally raise a minor hand gesture.

Release yourself from your binds and let your body speak for you. Place your notes on the podium and move away from it. Do this right after the previous speaker has been clutched to it, and your audience will get excited, because they can sense that you have the confidence to tell them the whole story -- using your hands and feet as well as your face and voice. They will be reading you and not just hearing what you say.

You should be able to get through your introduction without having to refer to your notes. Then, when you need to refer to notes, walk over to the podium and get reacquainted with them. This is not rude, but a short break from the openness that the audience likes. They would rather have you stand in front of them, allowing them to see what you are saying and occasionally glancing at your notes, than see your head nodding up and down over a podium.

Walking away from the protective podium may feel uncomfortable at first, but if you remember to stand relaxed and natural, you will get used to it. In fact, it may soon feel uncomfortable and awkward to stand behind a podium.

Coordinate With Other Speakers

When you are only one of multiple speakers on the agenda, try to get the outlines of the other speakers. Ideally, you want to do this before you begin preparing your presentation. But good luck! Since many presentations are put together at the last minute, asking someone for an outline a week in advance of the presentation, may be asking for too much.

If possible, get the group of speakers together for a meeting to discuss the need for a common theme across presentations. Also, look for opportunities to create transition from one presentation to the next. Spending a little group time upfront will have a dramatic impact on the outcome of each presentation.

Statements to Avoid

There are some statements that are extra wordy and unnecessary or ambiguous and have an adverse effect on your presentation. Here is a short list of them:

1. **"As some of you may know."** There are a few phrases that are completely unnecessary. This is often used when the speaker is

familiar with some of the audience members but not all. There is no difference between a sentence that includes that opening and the sentence that does not include that opening. For example, "As many of you know I am the Director of Operations..." is the same as "I am the director of operations...."

2. **"This may be familiar to some of you."** Again, these are unnecessary words if you know some of the audience may have some basic knowledge. Instead say something along the lines of "I will be starting off with a review of some basic concepts of..." When you tell them that your material may be familiar to them some of the audience members will sit back in their chairs and probably check their smartphones, but if you mention you will do a quick review, you will maintain engagement with your audience.

3. **"I want to tell you about"** This statement just adds some extra words. If you **want** to tell them, just tell them. The word "want" is the misplaced word in this statement and is passive, like you are not sure you really want to tell them. Consider the statement "I want to tell you about the future of blockchain technology" as compared to "Let me tell you about the future of blockchain technology" or "The future of blockchain technology is" The first one is passive and unconvincing. The second and third ones are more direct. Which one sounds more authoritative to you?

Avoid the Use of NONWORDS

A nonword is a "Sound filler," and not necessarily a word. Nonwords include "Ah," "Uhm," "Well," "You know." They have no place in your presentation because they detract from its quality.

Using nonwords is frustrating to the audience. Inevitably, there will be members of the audience who become so annoyed they start counting the number of nonwords you use.

The amazing part of the nonword problem is that most speakers do not realize they say them. One speaker I worked with was focusing on avoiding nonwords and speaking at the right speed. I watched and when he was done, I asked him how he did. He evaluated himself as speaking too slowly but he was pleased he did not use any nonwords. In actuality, the speaker's speed was perfect -- and he used over 30 nonwords in only 10 minutes.

The best way to avoid using nonwords is to listen to what you say as you say it. This is a hard habit to break because nonwords are spoken without realizing it. Correcting this flaw takes focused concentration and effort.

Through an informal survey, I have discovered that avid users of nonwords, often come from large families. The reason is that, in many large families, speaking is a competition. When someone has the floor, they can talk as long as something is coming out of their mouth. Once they pause, others start talking. The nonword acts as a placeholder for the speaker to gather thoughts. Although this may be necessary at the dinner table, it is detrimental to a presentation to a sophisticated audience. If a speaker needs to gather his or her thoughts in front of a group, the best thing to do is pause and be silent.

Use the Dramatic Pause

"Silence is the ultimate weapon of power." – Charles de Gaulle

Where nonwords can be damaging, pauses can be powerful. They can be used most effectively in two specific instances. The first is when the speaker just takes a pause to gather thoughts, organize slides or notes, or just change gears to another topic. The second is the dramatic pause.

The dramatic pause is deliberately inserted at a critical point to allow the audience to feel the impact of a hard-hitting statement. It gives them time to think about what you've just said, before listening to something new.

It can be a good idea to insert a dramatic pause at the end of one of your rhetorical questions posed to the audience. Pause and count. Three to five seconds is a good pause, but some can go as long as ten seconds. Give the audience ample time to ponder your statement.

Mini Pauses

Mini pauses are called periods. Avoid running all your sentences together. Speak with a good speed and pause at the period.

Judging your speed can be a difficult task. But if you cannot change to a faster speed, you are probably talking too fast. If you cannot effectively transition to emphasize a point or a word, you are probably going too fast. The best way to determine if you are going too slow is to videotape yourself giving your presentation and then watch it back.

Never Apologize

Never apologize for anything. If you get up in the front of the room and start off by telling the audience that you only had 1 day to prepare so you are not sure how this is going to go, you will put yourself in a hole that is impossible to get out of. When you apologize for being sick, being late, being tired, being unprepared, losing your place, you are just setting the stage for the audience to expect your failure. Be confident, roll with the punches and make the best of it, no matter the hurdles.

It's Okay to Have Minor Problems (You're Only Human)

Conducting a flawless presentation every time you speak is impossible. There will be times when an unexpected question or event will cause you to momentarily lose your place. This happens. In fact, an audience may welcome the slip as a sign that you are human.

If you need to go back to your notes or need to take a few moments to figure out where you are at, do it. Refer to your notes and resume when you have it all straightened out in your head. In informal, friendly situations, you might ask your audience "Where was I?" Of course, you run the risk that the audience will not remember where you were either (hence, they were not listening). Then you have to refer to your notes and figure it out on your own anyway.

Do Not Alienate Your Audience

Backgrounds and experiences are different, origins are different, and perceptions are different. When you speak, you do not want to alienate your audience by making references to one particular social group or another, either in a negative or positive way.

If you want to make reference to race, gender, nationality, or politics, rethink the need to include the comment. If you have re-evaluated it and you determine that you still need to include it, make sure you package it correctly. This is tough because each circumstance is different. The way to package a sensitive statement is to structure it so that the audience does not know your position after your statement, even though you have made your point. For example, if you want to make a reference to a politician's policy that you feel will have a negative impact on your company, you need to package it like the following: "I know our President is trying to balance the needs of many when developing his policies, but his tax policies will reduce our net income by X% and will limit our ability for growth." Structured this way, the audience cannot tell if you are a supporter for the President's party and are just displeased with this one policy or are against all of the policies of this President. When your comment is packaged correctly, you appear to be an independent unbiased person that objectively evaluates each and every policy.

Practice, Practice and Practice

"It usually takes me more than three weeks to prepare a good impromptu speech." -- Mark Twain

The difference between a great presentation and a mediocre presentation, is practice. Organizing your thoughts and preparing your slides is a good first step. But if you do not perform at least one practice run, you are destined to have flaws.

Practice lets you hear how your words sound. It will help you identify things that just do not fit together well, words that are used too many times, contradictory statements, redundant points, and slides that really do not fit with your main theme. Practice is remarkable. It takes things that look perfect on paper and exposes them for what they really are - a collection of thoughts that may not be tied with a common theme. Practice is the best way to make sure the magical journey of your presentation is being delivered to your audience the way you intended and is delivering the impact you wanted.

Practice helps you make smooth transitions from one topic to the next. If you know your material, you will do fine addressing each topic individually without a lot of practice. The transitions from one topic to another is where practice can work out the kinks. You can plan a mini-introduction for your next topic at the end of the previous topic.

Practice in front of a mirror at least once before each presentation. The mirror will help you identify any distracting body language, poor posture or awkward hand movements or placements. It is also a constant reminder to smile and keep your head up.

Without practice, it is difficult to perform your planned body moves correctly in your presentation. The first time you run through your presentation, your focus is usually on content. You don't want that first time to be in front of your audience. Practice, practice and practice until you get the right inflection in your voice at the right time and your body motions are in sync with your points.

Rehearse Your Presentation Length

I am surprised how many times I have seen presentations that are much shorter or much longer than the allotted time. If you have to fill 20 minutes, make sure you have not prepared a presentation that will run 40 minutes or 10 minutes, although it's better to be shorter than longer. It is inconsiderate to the audience and the event coordinators that expect you to fill a 20-minute slot and then you run over. Practice your timing using a clock or stopwatch, and make sure you are not going to be over your time slot. Target being short so you have time for questions, without going over.

I recommend using a stopwatch and noting the times at various points throughout your presentation. This allows you to see which sections may need to be cut and provides you with a guide when you are doing your actual presentation. If you come to the halfway point in your presentation and you are more than halfway through your allotted time, you can adjust the remainder of your presentation to shorten it or maybe spend less time explaining the charts.

It is not uncommon for your presentation length to be adjusted shorter or longer on the day of your presentation by your event coordinator. What do you do if you have prepared a 30-minute presentation and then you are told that you will have only 15 minutes for your topic? To prepare for this, go through your presentation and identify what can be cut out in case that happens to you. If you are using a slideshow presentation, have a shorter presentation file with certain slides hidden, in case you have to fill a shorter timeslot.

What about being asked to fill a longer time slot? First, you can identify areas in your slides where you can embellish more, but that is not ideal. If you are scheduled for 30 minutes and the coordinator tells you that you must fill the entire hour, you should change your presentation to engage the audience more. Start off with your same introduction and then ask them to identify some of the key points they want to cover. You can guide them through this process, essentially getting them to the same point but with some interactivity. To add more time, set specific breaks in the middle of your presentation to field questions on the previous section.

I was once asked to attend a 2-day conference and observe the participants and the speakers. I showed up at 6:30 am to have breakfast with the two people responsible for the agenda, but they had no agenda. I could not believe it. People flew in from all over the country to attend this 2-day event, and the facilitators had no agenda. They told me it was supposed to be a working session and they wanted someone to lead it. Someone independent that nobody had seen before. They both looked at me as I ate my omelet. At that moment I realized I had 2 hours to come up with an agenda for the entire day. I figured I could worry about the second day if I survived the first day.

I started the session off with a relevant quote about the importance of keeping an eye on the competition and continually improving our products. Luckily, the quote came from a book that I read on the flight to this conference. I then broke the day into sections to make it extremely interactive. The first section was listening to the sales agents talk about what competitors were offering that we weren't. The second section was analyzing and prioritizing the importance of these differences. We literally had a dozen flipcharts taped all over the walls with this new information. After lunch, we took the critical approach and analyzed our current products and identified what improvements the salespeople thought we needed to make it easier for them to secure the sale. This comprised another half dozen flipcharts. We then narrowed it down to the top five product improvements and then created a presentation to management on these changes. The final section of the day was a group presentation from the sales agents to the management of the company. Several of the proposed changes were implemented, which resulted in some significant increases in revenue and ultimate an entirely new line of business. At the end of the day, I was exhausted, but I had a great time, and the meeting participants said it was one of the most productive meetings they ever had. The second day was a lot easier since I had an entire evening to prepare.

Working With Your Notes

Never staple your notes together. It makes it awkward when you flip to the next page. Leave your sheets. When you are done with one page, you can simply slide it to the side to go to the next page.

If you need help with your actions, you may want to make signposts on your notes to indicate when to use dramatic pauses, faster or slower speech, louder or softer tone, gestures or visual aids. This will make sure you do not forget to add that extra impact to your presentation.

The key to organizing content is the "Primary Point Pyramid" method, as described in the following section.

Primary Point Pyramid Method

The Primary Point Pyramid method of content development includes the following steps:

1. Identify the primary points you want to cover in your presentation.
2. Identify the main theme that ties the points together.
3. List under each primary point, the sub points you want to make.
4. List the visual aids required to reinforce each primary point.
5. Develop your introduction and conclusion.
6. Add emphasis to key points

1. *Identify the primary points you want to cover in your presentation.*

   In a financial presentation for example, the primary points could be sales, cost of sales, operating expenses, net earnings, inventories and return on equity. In a sales presentation the primary points could be product benefits, strength and stability of company, integrity of management, responsiveness of customer service, and reliability of products.

Identifying these primary points is the easiest part of developing your presentation. The difficulty comes in tying these points together with a main theme.

2. *Identify the main theme that ties the points together.*

The most crucial step in developing the structure of your content is identifying a single unified theme. The thought that you can't have more than one main theme is tough for some to accept, but it must be done. The main theme may be closer to one of the primary points than the others. For example, see the section on "Identifying the common theme."

To develop your main theme, list your primary points and ask yourself: What is it that the points have in common? What direction are all the points heading in? What ties them all together? Sometimes you must look really hard to find a common bond. If you can't find it, perhaps some of your primary points should be left for another presentation. The presidential candidates always have a common theme that they keep referring to. For example, they may talk about the need for welfare reform, health care reform, balanced budget, crime fighting, affirmative action, and tie it all together with a common theme that they are "sensitive to the needs of the people and will do what is best for the country." They really stretch it far to tie it all together. Hopefully, you can find a closer bond.

Using the example in Step 1, if your main topics are sales, cost of sales, operating expenses, net earnings, inventories and return on equity, your main point could be that your new marketing program has had a remarkable impact on the results of the Company. Then, when you talk about the individual topics, you indicate how the marketing plan impacted each.

Step 2 - Identifying Main Theme

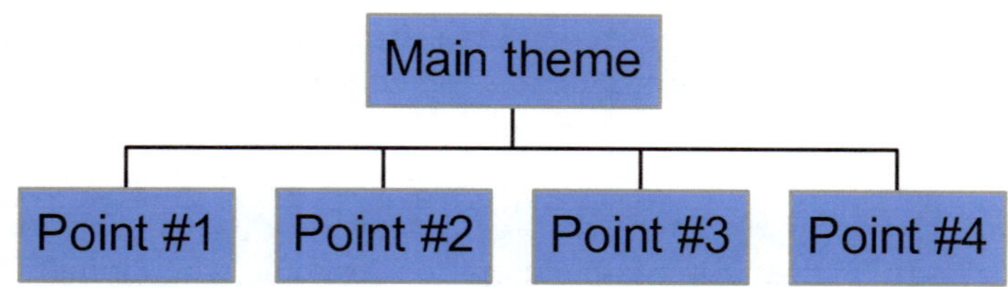

3. *List under each point, the sub points you want to make.*

Now that you have identified your primary points and main theme, identify what you want to cover under each of the primary points. Remember your main theme as you list the sub points. All the sub points listed under each point do not have to be directly related to the main theme. However, the main theme needs to be kept in mind as you develop your sub points to keep your theme focused. For example, suppose your sales presentation's main theme is the importance of good customer service. This theme should be reflected in most of the sub points. You can cover all your primary points while continuing to reinforce that main theme within each sub point.

Step 3 - Adding subpoints

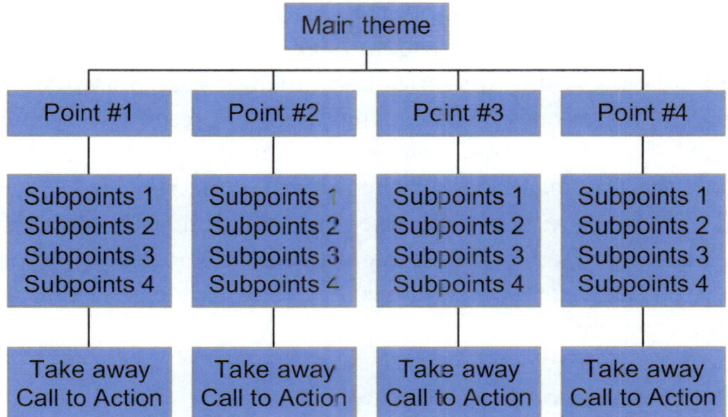

Reinforcing good customer service in a sales presentation can easily be stressed in the primary point on product benefits. Also, you can stress that good customer service has led to the strength and stability of the company. Customer service can also be touted as a main philosophy of management and covered in the point on the integrity of management. If you can sell the customer service angle in all your primary points, you will have a leg up on the competition and likely will make your sales.

For presentations designed to sway the audience toward your point of view, the sub points should stress your position on the topic, why you believe it, and what you expect the audience to do. Avoid presenting both sides of the issue without firmly committing what you believe. The audience prefers to know where you stand. Otherwise, they will think you are wishy-washy or afraid to take a stance. Let your audience hear your point of view.

4. *List the visual aids required to reinforce each primary point.*

After identifying the primary points, your main theme, and your sub points to support your main theme, you can determine where you need additional support to reinforce your statements. This reinforcement is typically in the form of visual aids, such as handouts, projection slides or other overheads.

Visual aids should be used to reinforce points that need to be substantiated with more than words. When you are talking about how profitable your company is, it is probably time to show a pro forma financial statement chart, table or graph. If you are talking technically about your products, you may want to display statistics to lend more credibility to your words.

To plan your visual aids, look at your primary points and your sub points, keeping your main theme in mind. Then identify the points and sub points that need support. Describe what information and type of visual aid would work best, so later, you can go back and create it. Avoid creating visuals first and then building your presentation around them. When visuals are prepared before presentation content, the speaker becomes a supporter or narrator of the slides and the slides become the dominant force in the presentation.

If you are using the sales presentation with our main theme "good customer service," you might use a slide on results of a customer survey, service call response times, or number of service calls compared to your competitor.

5. *Develop your introduction and conclusion*

If you have adequately carried out the first four steps of this process, developing the introduction should be relatively easy. If you have not done your job in the first four steps, preparing your introduction will be difficult.

Introductions should be timely. Scan the current events in the newspaper and on the morning news shows for topics and situations that can be assimilated into your main theme and used in your introduction. The introduction does not have to be complicated. For example, I heard this one which was very effective in an acquisition presentation:

> "Did you see this morning's paper? A truck was passing under an overpass, but it was too tall because of the low clearance of the bridge. The truck got stuck. The city had engineers, policeman and fireman trying to figure out how to get the truck out from under the bridge. They determined that they could not lift the bridge and could not free the truck. Then a small boy watching suggested letting the air out of the tires, hence lowering the truck to allow it to fit under the bridge. A simple solution. During this acquisition process we were in a few tight situations ourselves and what we needed was a simple solution

to allow us to come to an agreement. I am glad to say, we have found one. Now..."

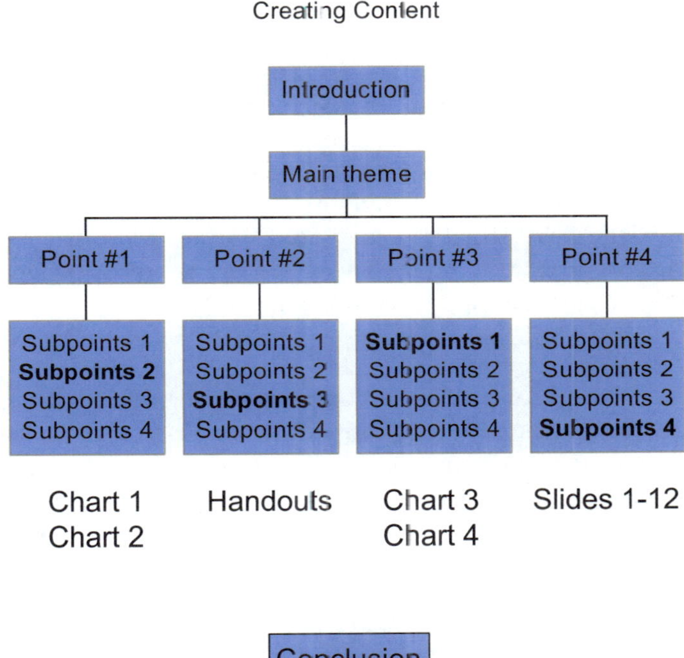

This introduction was very quick, but effective, because it is interesting and provided an important point. It demonstrated that there are often simple solutions to seemingly difficult problems.

The conclusion is the distribution of the audience's marching orders. It is a crucial part of the presentation. This is your last chance to convey your main theme. You started off with it, you reinforced it throughout the presentation, now you want it to be the last thing they hear before the audience leaves. All they need now are action items for follow up.

If you had them captivated and listening intently throughout your presentation, your best chance of getting action as a result of your presentation is to identify and assign them as part of your conclusion. Assigning action items days after a presentation will result in a lower enthusiasm level towards their completion.

The best way to accomplish this is to begin your conclusion with another synopsis or your presentation's key points or another thought-provoking story which relates directly to and supports your main theme. Hammering home your main theme in one all-encompassing summary will get the audience eager to perform their specific action items.

For example, a presentation made by a software engineer who is recommending the switch, should include the summary of the key benefits of the product and a list of concerns raised by the audience during the presentation. To get closure on this recommendation, action items associated with the necessary follow up to resolve issues and concerns raised by the audience should be assigned with dates as part of the conclusion. Otherwise, the software recommendation will be shelved, and another meeting may be required to get closure. By identifying what specific items need to be addressed and upon satisfactory resolution of the issues, we can proceed to purchase the product without having to reconvene the group.

6. *Add emphasis and stress points*

   Once your pyramid is complete, revisit and highlight the areas where you want to add emphasis. This emphasis may be other than where you support your points with visual aids. For example, new ideas and bold statements probably will need a special delivery. Nothing extreme, just some voice inflection, change of speed or volume, or good hand and / or body gestures.

Finally, make a clean, clear copy of your pyramid as a one-page document. It will provide a good reference guide to help you deliver your presentation more effectively. If you have practiced your presentation enough, this document could be all the notes you will need.

Some final tips:

Using sticky notes for each of the boxes when building your pyramid will allow you to rearrange your thoughts to get the best order and flow in your presentation. Also, it limits the amount of material you can write in each box, forcing you to focus your presentation.

Reinforce your main theme throughout your presentation by developing a one liner. For example, if your main theme is unparalleled customer service, you might use a line throughout your presentation like this: "Our Company is committed to providing you the quality products and related services you deserve!" Then whenever you complete a topic, you can throw that line in. This technique is very powerful for getting your point across and is used by many successful speakers.

Leave Behinds and Handouts

The last step in the preparation is to define your leave behinds. A leave behind is exactly that, what you will be leaving behind when you complete your presentation. It is never acceptable to leave behind your entire slide deck. Your slide deck should contain bullets and phrases that do not stand alone because they are supporting you and your presentation and without you, they are not providing the entire story. Leaving the slides without you as the narrator will be confusing or uninformative to the reader, especially if they give a copy to someone else that did not attend the presentation. Instead, consider these alternatives to complete slides:

1. A high-level summary is typically a one pager that summarizes the key points, findings and take-aways with little supporting details. This is the preferred leave behind for your presentation.

2. The detailed synopsis is a complete list of all support for your presentation. This is not something you would tend to leave behind, especially for external audiences. If you are making a financial presentation and you have charts and graphs, some of the audience may be so inclined as to want to see the detail behind the summary results.

3. The key point summary is a combination of the images and slides used, but with some explanation. This would include bullets that are not just one or two words, but full sentences to explain the bullets. This expanded version is required since you are not going home with them to narrate the slides. Plus, it will include some of your other comments and explanations that you spoke about that are not readily surmised through the slides themselves. This is a separate and distinct set of slides from your presentation slide deck.

4. Another potential leave behind is a summary of the discussion that ensued during the meeting. This is more typical when it is less of a presentation and more of an interactive discussion. In more formal meetings with upper management and board members, this could be in the form of minutes. Often these discussion summaries are documented during the meeting, then cleaned up afterwards and sent to the parties subsequently. They often include action items for later follow up.

5. If you are giving a sales presentation, you should leave behind some brochures of your products and your company. If you have any marketing giveaways like pens, leave those behind as well. If a pen has your company name on it, every time they use it, they will see your company name and logo, which is a good for name recognition and reinforcement.

7. LOGISTICS ARE IMPORTANT

As mentioned before, most speakers spend the majority of their time preparing their content. Few spend the appropriate amount of time on the visual aspects of their presentation. When it comes to the logistics - lighting, equipment, podium, audio visual equipment, temperature - few take the time to assure they are working properly.

Consider this nightmare scenario: After departing with what you thought was ample time to get to your presentation, you get stuck in gridlock traffic and show up late. Then you have problems getting your video projector to work. The room layout does not allow for your planned movements, the room is 85° and the lighting is wrong for your overheads. In this scenario, even a high interest presentation will have many strikes against it. The audience expects things to go right, and if they don't, they think you have not prepared enough.

Show Up Early

To avoid the above scenario, show up at the presentation location early. Check the temperature and locate the thermostat in case it must be adjusted later when warm bodies fill the room. Next, check the lighting, to make sure it is right for your presentation. Adjust the lights to the way you want them during your presentation and walk around the room to make sure there are no visibility problems. Once you're satisfied, note the position of the light switches in case you must make a later adjustment - especially if you will be following somebody that is using a different lighting scheme.

Most importantly, check your audio-visual equipment. How do you turn it on? Does the projection bulb work? Is there a spare? How is the spare installed? Where does it plug in? How do you focus it? Do you have to plug your computer or other components into it?

Look at the layout of the room and determine if it is sufficient to allow you to move the way you planned. If not, see if you can change it. If the room is classroom style - rows of chairs and tables all facing forward - and you need a more interactive set up to allow the audience to see each other - change it. You are not going to be confident unless you are satisfied with the layout of the room and all the other logistics are the way you want them.

For example, a speaker showed up early to make sure his equipment was set up but did not check anything else. As people filed in and the room filled up, the speaker just waited. When it came time to start, the speaker took to the front of the room, but found there was not much room to move. Then when the projector was turned on, he found he could not stand in front of the room without blocking some of the projected images. When he stood off to the side, part of the audience could not hear him.

It was entertaining to watch him try to resolve the situation. The projector was in the aisle, directly in front of a support column. The only place for the speaker to stand was directly behind the column at the back of the room. When he faced forward, he faced the column. When he spoke to one side or the other, the other side could not hear him. The audience either looked straight ahead to view the slides or turned completely around to see the speaker. The result was a disaster.

When the room layout is set, check for sound. If you originally planned on 30 people and now 300 are expected to show up, secure a microphone. Or, if the acoustics of the room absorb sound with a planned small group, you may need to consider a microphone. To be safe, always plan for a microphone in case you need it, unless you are familiar with the location and have experience in that particular setting.

Show up early and make sure your logistics are right -- and you will be well on your way to a successful presentation.

Nutrition - Avoid Dehydrating Foods

To be confident in your presentation, you need to be comfortable. Being too hot, too cold, dehydrated, overstuffed or hungry are not states you want to be in during your presentation.

Avoid eating a big meal directly before your presentation, but do not perform on an empty stomach either. When you do eat before a presentation, avoid foods that may cause indigestion or dehydration. This includes spicy, salty, or greasy fried foods.

Dehydration is a major concern. It is said that the two most dehydrating activities for people are flying and speaking. So, if you are flying to a speaking engagement, you need to take extra care.

The key to avoid dehydration is to drink water, and plenty of it. Plan to have a glass of water available when you speak, but do not drink so much that you need to take a bathroom break in the middle of your presentation.

Foods that cause dehydration include caffeine (coffee, soda and tea), concentrated sweets (candy, juice and sodas) and alcohol. It is best to avoid these items for at least 12 hours before you speak.

8. PRESENTING WITH VISUAL AIDS

There are speeches and there are presentations. One major difference is the use of visual aids. Speeches tend to be made from a podium and can vary in crowd size, and usually do not include any visual aids. Presentations where you are presenting an idea to a targeted audience with a specific objective and call to action may include visual aids to help you to make your case. Presentation aids can help you explain and support the information and the claims you make in your presentation. There is no better way to illustrate a point then to use a well-placed image, chart, or graph. Common visual aids include flipcharts, whiteboards, computer slides, models and props and handouts. Public speaking using audio and visual aids is an art. As discussed in earlier chapters, if you execute all the basics, including identifying and maintaining your main theme, standing tall, talking loudly and clearly, and maintaining eye contact with your audience, your probability of a successful speech will be high. When you incorporate visual aids, you add a whole new series of factors that affect your success ratio. These factors include properly transitioning between slides, giving your audience time to absorb your slide before speaking, maintaining a reasonable number of slides, establishing where to stand while the slides are presented, making sure the content is right for the audience and your topic, and using the correct colors and typeface. This may all sound academic, but in reality, these items usually are not addressed until the actual presentation is taking place.

The Purpose of Visual Aids

The best way to make a presentation is to tell a story. An interconnected set of lines that leads the audience on a magical journey to win them over to your perspective and ultimately get them to respond to your call to action. Your story must be compelling and the claims that you make during your journey must be supported by facts and truths. If you make a claim that sales are going to increase over the next 4 quarters because of several reasons including the trend set over the past year, you better have a supporting chart to show that trend. It's not that the audience will not believe you, it's just that when you say it and they hear it, and then they can see it, they become convinced. This gets us to our first point on presenting data: repetition

Repetition Is the Key to Learning

Have you ever noticed on radio commercials where they repeat the phone number a dozen times in 30 seconds? This is a little overkill and I feel frustrated after the commercial is over, but the point is, the more your repeat your message, the more it will be remembered. This is not a recommendation to repeat your statements, rather to create supporting slides that essentially repeat or support the statements you make.

Message Redundancy

Message redundancy is when you convey your point in different ways. You may speak to it in one or two ways, then show a chart or graph or image to support what you said. This pounds home the point without being repetitively verbatim. Remember, there are different types of learners in the audience, and you want appeal to those that are auditory learners as well as visual learners, fast learners as well as slower learners. When you show a chart, you should also use a chart title that embeds your message as well. If you are showing a chart of sales for 4 quarters, the title should not be "Sales for the past 4 quarters" it should be something like "Sales growth trend" which supports more closely the point about increasing sales you are trying to make. The chart title is interpreting the data rather than just labeling it. When you do it this way, the audience reads the title – essentially the conclusion of the data and then reads the chart to see what supports that statement or title. This is data redundancy

Relevance and Scale

Sometimes when creating a slide presentation, the presenter can get a little carried away and incorporate slides that probably don't belong, but the presenter found them and thought they would be great to share with the audience. Maybe they found some great information about a customer support survey that shows the company has stellar customer support. This is a great piece of information that must be shared with the entire organization, but if your presentation is about improving a production line with new equipment or an analysis of sales by type, it is not relevant to the point being presented and should be excluded.

When you create a slide, make sure you are speaking the same language as your audience. If you are talking with upper management, they will know what ROI, EBITAB and EPS are, but others in the company may not have any idea what those acronyms mean. Your slides should also use labels and titles that are relevant to your audience.

Using a relevant scale is important too. If you look at the Profit Margin Trends Charts, they both represent the same exact data, except the one on the left has a scale starting at 20% and the one on the right starts at 0%. Visually, looking at the slide on the left, one might conclude that the Commercial and Government lines are not profitable, but when you look at the slide on the right, these lines are clearly profitable. Make sure your scale on the graph does not distort your message.

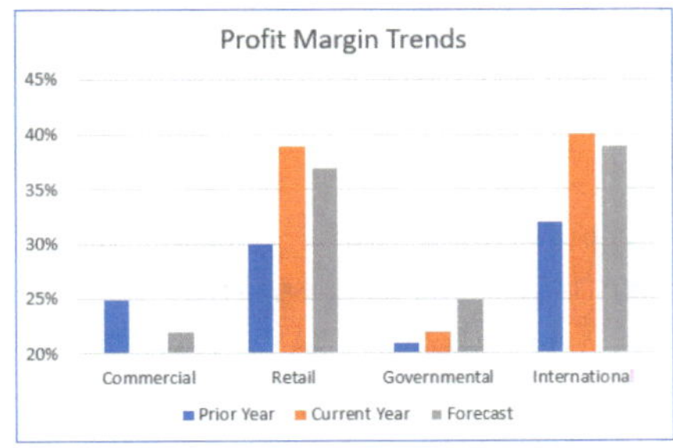

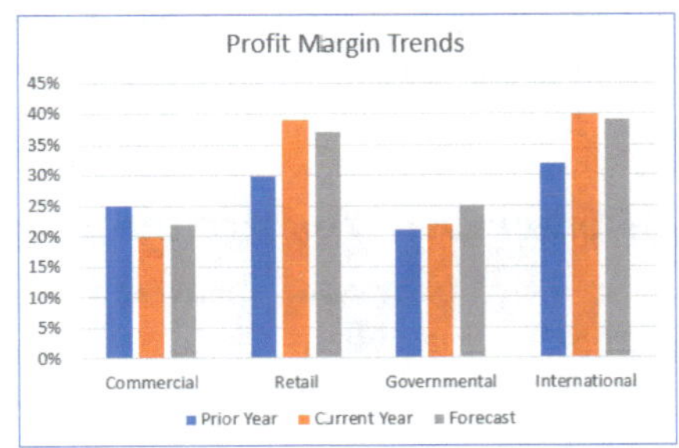

Visual Consistency

Visual Consistency is especially important for your presentation. If you are showing some financial charts and comparing the current year with the prior year and showing a forecast, make sure that in each graph the colors remain the same for each category of data throughout your presentation. For example, if the forecast is gray on one slide, the forecast should be gray on all slides. The same with prior year and current year numbers as well. That makes it easier on the audience and you want them to be relaxed so they can focus on your key points, your message and your call to action.

Presenting with Images and Videos

"They say a picture is worth a thousand words, but if those thousand words were spoken, no one would remember them." – David W. Kolakowski

People are likely to remember a story if it is associated with an image than if they just heard the point. Based on studies done, when information is presented orally without pictures, only 10% will remember it after 3 days. The brain is NOT designed to store text, as words are manmade constructs. Images have a much higher impact than just text or words. Images make learning more memorable and more engaging, so it is a great way for you to get your point across. You can communicate better if the audience can store a picture and associate it with the point you are trying to make. Images to include are drawings, clipart, pictures and designs. Certain concepts are more easily conveyed using images and videos. For example, if you described in words how to caulk a window it might take you 10 minutes, and the retention rate would be near zero. But if you showed a 30 second video or even a picture, you could convey that knowledge quickly and easily, with a high retention rate.

Use images to create some drama, get some reaction from your audience and prepare them to listen to your points and then they will act on your call to action.

Remember: You Are the Speaker

You are the speaker, and you are the presenter. Do not rely on the presentation aids to take center focus. You are not there to be a narrator to your slides. The purpose of your visual aids is to project a professional image. You may look professional and be totally prepared for your speech, but adding professional looking slides, props or handouts or facilitating an interactive flipchart or whiteboard session will raise your image.

Not only does it add to your professionalism, but it also adds to your credibility. When you make a statement and then support it with an image or other visual, you back up your statement and it opens the eyes of your audience acknowledging that you are indeed the expert in this field. When you use interactive visuals like a flipchart or whiteboard you engage the audience and they become an integral part of your presentation. Lastly, when you incorporate a visual aid that contains facts, charts or sources, it helps to explain your position and educate your audience.

When selecting your visual aids, ask these three questions about each and every chart or graphic you are considering:

1. Does it reinforce the main theme?

Your goal for the presentation is to stick to one common theme. Does this graphic support the main idea? Or is it just some good information that you think the audience wants to know?

Ideally, you want your slides to have one main image on it, so that it makes an impact and supports the idea you are discussing. When the idea is simple, the impact can be supported with a single image, but in many business presentations there are financial slides that contain numbers, charts and graphs that cannot easily be conveyed in a single picture. Case in point, if you have an app for iPhone and you want to show how easy it is to use, accomplish this by showing a picture of some people happily using the app. The following section will focus on making more affective business and financial slides.

Often in business presentations, a business analyst will create 30-40 performance graphs and charts, showing everything from market share to sales by employee to sales trends by state. The speaker then takes the graphics and builds the presentation around them. What typically results is a presentation of graphic and charts on slides with a few words in between. Graphics are meant to support your main theme, not draw attention away from it.

First identify your major points and the main theme, compose the outline, identify what graphics are needed, and then develop the graphics (See discussion of Primary Point Pyramid method in a previous chapter).

The best time to use slides to support a point is right after you make a strong or controversial statement. For example, if you are discussing a business strategy that you state will add $2 million to the bottom line, the audience will expect a detailed chart to support your estimate.

Using statistics and numbers adds credibility to your presentation, especially if the audience questions your knowledge or expertise. Cite your sources when statistics are used. See cited sources below:

Relationship to Householder by Age: 2010

(For information on confidentiality protection, nonsampling errors, and definitions, see *www.census.gov/prod/cen2010/doc/sf1.pdf*)

Relationship type	Total	Number				
		Under 18 years	18 to 29 years	30 to 44 years	45 to 64 years	65 years and over
Total household population	**300,758,215**	**73,920,881**	**47,903,506**	**59,766,531**	**80,357,019**	**38,810,278**
Householder	116,716,292	28,297	13,862,048	30,758,709	46,247,402	25,819,836
Spouse	56,510,377	8,793	4,863,702	17,524,307	24,935,103	9,178,472
Biological son or daughter	82,582,058	60,466,596	16,007,784	3,941,728	2,093,818	72,132
Adopted son or daughter	2,072,312	1,527,020	403,558	99,376	41,282	1,076
Stepson or stepdaughter	4,165,886	2,784,531	1,100,511	217,220	61,226	2,398
Brother or sister	3,433,951	298,242	1,125,419	848,247	922,338	239,705
Father or mother	3,033,003	(X)	(X)	128,343	1,187,041	1,717,619
Grandchild	7,139,601	5,825,229	1,117,324	180,096	16,926	26
Parent-in-law	925,713	(X)	(X)	10,178	281,266	634,269
Son-in-law or daughter-in-law	1,216,299	25,063	593,674	428,186	158,997	10,379
Other relative	4,662,672	1,631,262	1,268,787	774,403	648,580	339,640
Roomer or boarder	1,526,210	142,899	559,814	376,180	363,573	83,744
Housemate or roommate	5,223,365	42,515	3,163,824	1,084,638	769,490	162,898
Unmarried partner	7,744,711	11,651	2,622,772	2,724,034	2,020,431	365,823
Other nonrelative	3,805,765	1,128,783	1,214,289	670,886	609,546	182,261

(X) Not applicable

Source: U.S. Census Bureau, *2010 Census Summary File 1.*

2. Does it Answer, "Compared to What?"

Showing information graphically is usually better than trying to explain it with words, as long as it does not raise more questions than it answers. Also, displaying single points or a few relative points of data does not show the audience the whole story, and sometimes can be misleading. For example, showing increased company earnings in each of the past five years looks great, but if the industry average is twice as high as yours, you are likely misleading your audience.

Always ask yourself if your slide could have more comparative information in it. Is your slide merely a presentation of facts or does it show how those facts compare to the past, the competitors, your targets, etc.? Can your slide be enhanced by adding another element? If we are showing a bar chart of earnings over five years, for example, does it compare the results with target earnings, with industry averages, your major competitors?

Similarly, information can be misleading if inter-related facts are presented on separate slides. The audience cannot be expected to remember a series of slides, assemble the information in their heads and draw conclusions, especially when the slides are moving on and off the screen quickly.

Consider the following example where ABC Company is making a presentation to its shareholders. Exhibits A-F demonstrate a single item data element per slide (not the recommended approach), and Exhibits G&H demonstrate how a completely different scenario becomes evident when one additional data element is added for comparison.

Exhibit A represents ABC Company sales in units for the last five years, increasing a remarkable 460% over five years.

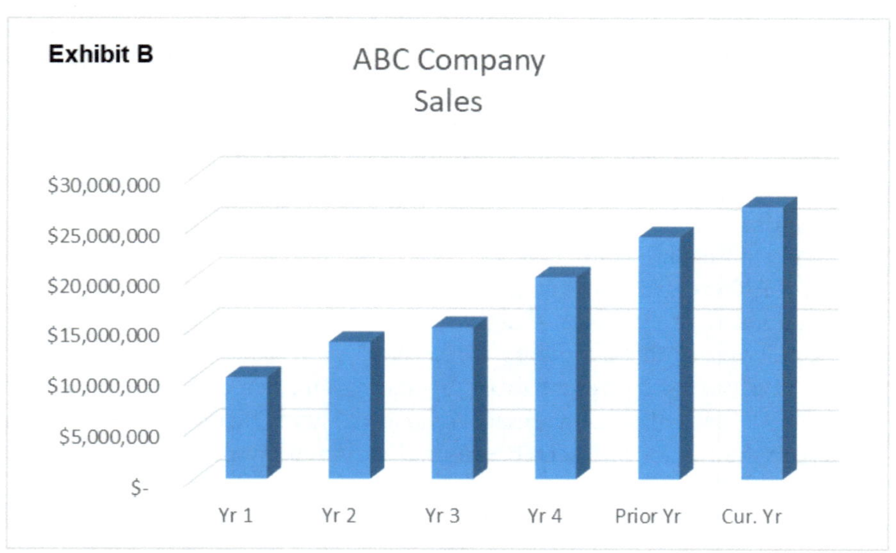

Exhibit B is the corresponding Sales dollar exhibit, which is also impressive. In a market where competition is heating up, they have been able to grow successfully.

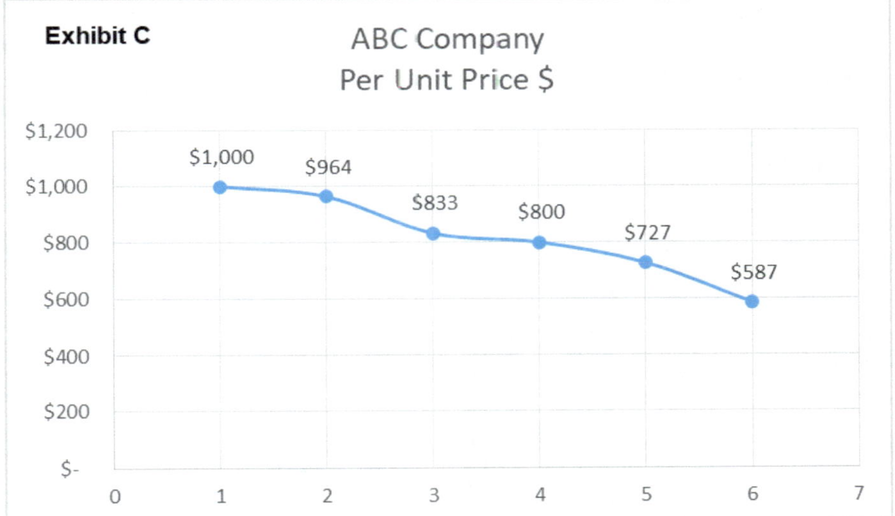

Exhibit C indicates that market and competitive forces have pushed prices down, but the company has been able to increase unit sales and sales dollars successfully. After all, the speaker explains, products enter the market at the highest price and continue to be produced more cheaply, hence reducing per unit sales price. The audience will likely remember the first three exhibits in a positive light.

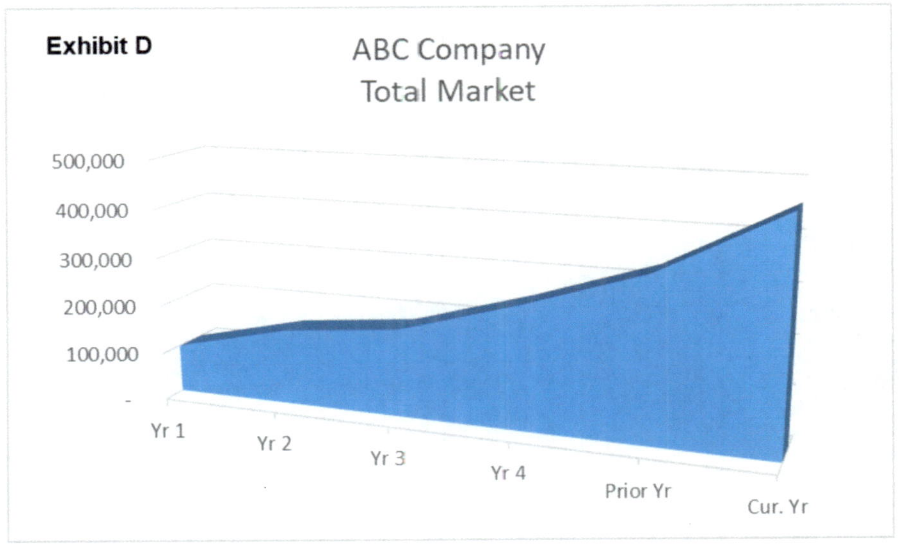

The presenter now switches to Exhibit D, an estimate of the total market. Exhibit D was tabulated from a research group and indicates that the company's potential for growth is vast. In fact, this market growth is faster than the company had anticipated and therefore, it was not able to build up appropriately to meet the potential market.

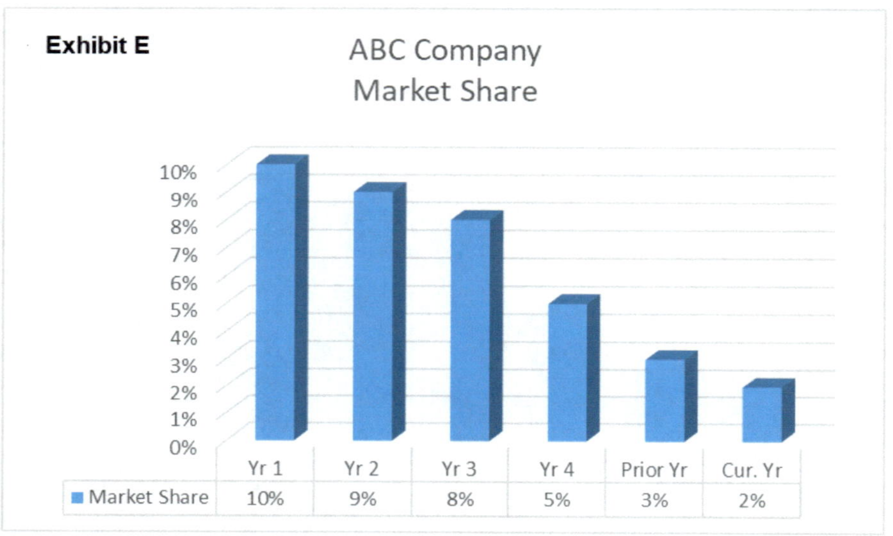

This is why Exhibit E shows a declining market share.

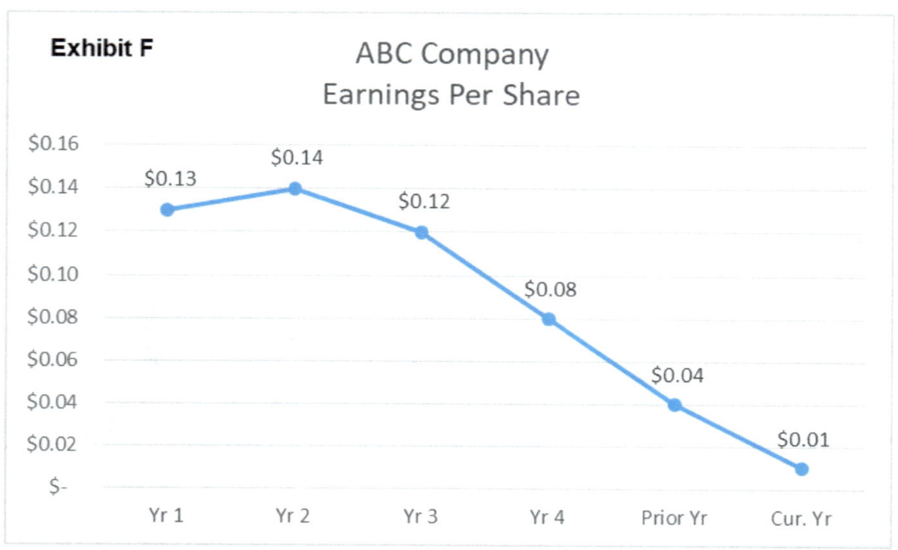

Quickly, the presenter moves to Exhibit F which shows a declining earnings per share cost and quips something about the need to ramp up expenses for the upsurge in market potential.

If the Exhibits go by fast enough, the audience will not really have time to relate one to the other or ask questions accordingly. They are stuck with one fact at a time and are influenced by the presenter's comments.

If the slides are too basic, or don't explain their inter-relationships, the audience may get frustrated with the presenter. Their questions will be left unanswered. The audience wants to analyze all the facts and be part of the presentation. Exhibits A-F are NOT the way to go.

Conversely, if we add comparative information to our examples above, we would be able to cover more topics in the same amount of time and get the audience involved. Exhibits G&H use the same information as Exhibits A-F yet transform the seemingly rosy picture into a more accurate depiction of the situation.

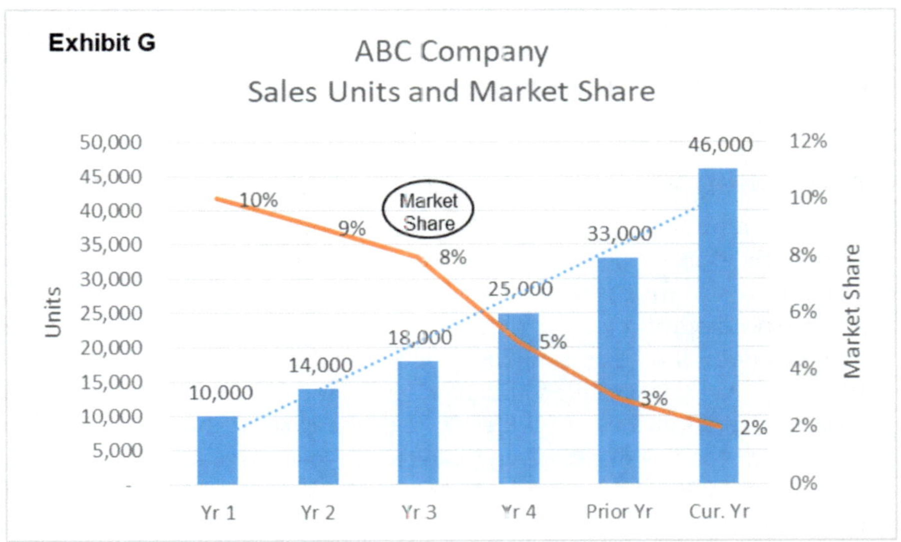

Suppose the speaker put Exhibit G on the projector and let the audience absorb it for a while (10 seconds). The increase in unit sales becomes a non-issue, and the concern becomes why ABC Company is losing substantial market share. Questions are immediately raised that would not be readily apparent in the first set of exhibits. Questions will raise issues ranging from marketing and advertising to quality and service. The audience instantly has increased participation and concern.

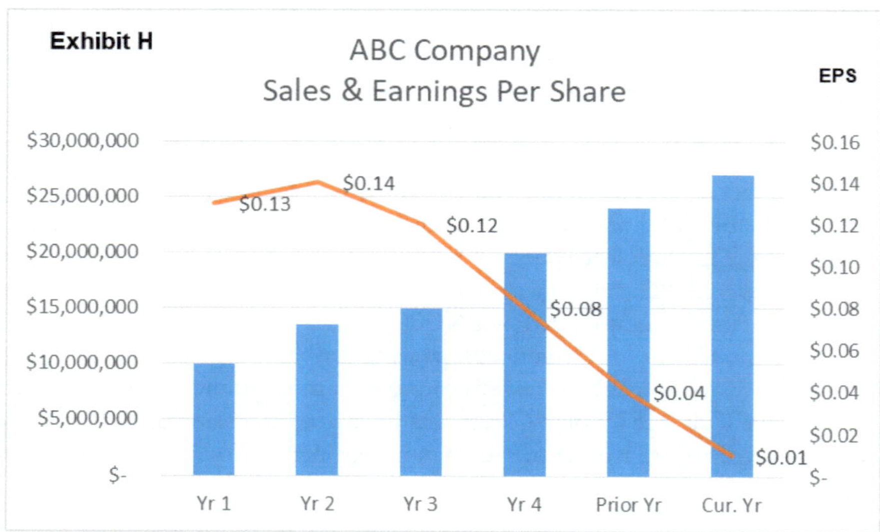

Exhibit H raises even more eyebrows. With the substantial increase in sales dollars, EPS is shrinking. Cost containment appears nonexistent. The audience has seen 2 exhibits and sees expenses out of control and not enough emphasis on maintaining market share.

Progressive Disclosure for Charts and Graphs

Unfortunately, showing charts G & H may confuse your audience because they have too much information on them. While giving them 6-10 seconds to absorb it is a nice gesture, there is a better way. If you use progressive disclosure on the slide, you can walk the audience through your thought process, so they completely understand what you are referring to. With your slide presentation software, show one piece of the data. Then explain what is on the screen. Then, with the click of the mouse another part of the chart is displayed and explain the new piece of data exposed. Do this until the chart is complete. This method assures that you don't lose your audience by displaying a confusing chart all at once.

3. Does Your Slide Show Results, Cause and Effect?

As in the example above, there were a lot of questions that would be raised by the audience when shown Exhibits G & H. Not only is it good to add multiple elements of related data to enhance the level of information on your slide, but it is also good to show some cause-and-effect information. Why did sales go up? Were there statistics available that would answer that question if placed on the slide to show the audience a cause-and-effect relationship? Some obvious relationships include an increase in earnings, which resulted from increased sales, maintaining cost of sales and controlling expenses (Exhibit I).

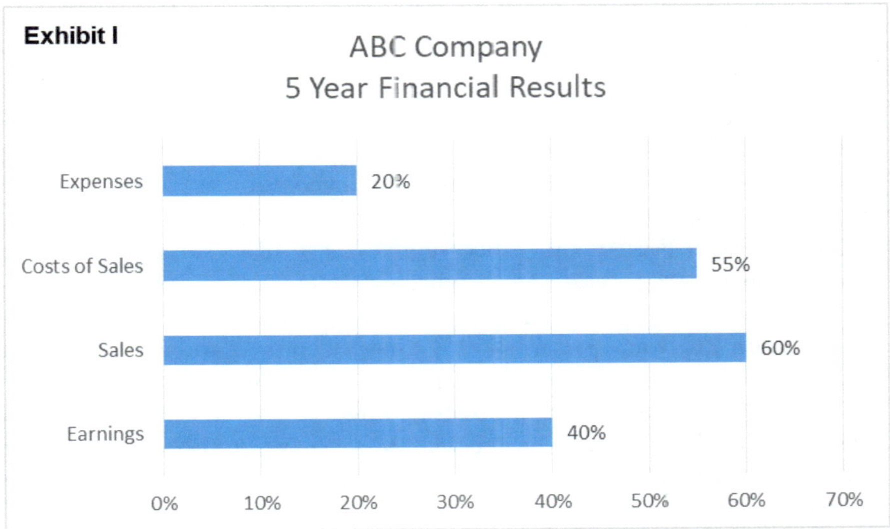

This chart shows why earning have gone up. It is not just because of sales, as the VP of marketing may claim. Nor is it just maintaining production costs, as the VP of operations would say. Nor is it just the controlling of expense increases, as the controller may conclude. It is a combination of all three. If any of the individual components were presented with earnings (without the other components), the audience would ask why the increase in earnings was not the same as the increase in sales, for example. The entire picture needs to be presented.

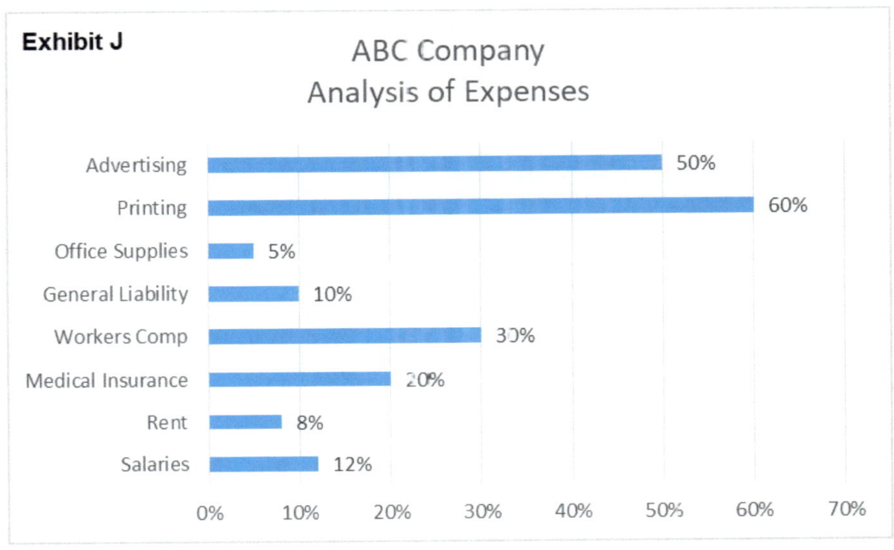

Exhibit J shows the detailed breakdown of the 20% change in expenses shown in Exhibit I. Without this level of breakdown some interesting information goes uncovered. For example, Exhibit I shows that expenses increased 20%. The conclusion may be drawn that they are under control, but Exhibit J shows that there are some areas that need looking into. Advertising, printing, and worker's compensation are areas that have increased significantly over the last five years. Slow increases in rent, salaries, general liability and office supplies have been sufficient to allow overall expenses to be viewed as "controlled."

Even nonfinancial cause-and-effect data will add good variety and information to your presentation. Information regarding changes in headcount, number of sales offices, number of prospect calls, market share comparisons and advertising responses, often add an interesting angle to your presentation. Your audience will know you've done your homework and have looked beyond the financial results. You'll create credibility as a broad thinker, not someone mired in just the financial numbers.

When developing visual aids continue to ask yourself "why?" each time you add another bit of information to your graph. For example, suppose you have a chart showing a 60% increase in sales over a five-year period (as in Exhibit I). Ask yourself "Why?" There is likely more than one answer. The increase in sales could be due to an increase in advertising and an increase in the number of prospect calls (since prospect calls turned into sales two out of every five times in Year 1 and two out of every four times in Year 5), you could include that on your chart. Then ask, why have prospect calls gone up? It may be because there are more people calling from more locations to a larger distribution area. If so ask "Why?" Maybe sales expanded into other countries. You can go on and on. After identifying all the possible "Why's," list them, and then determine which ones would have the greatest meaning to your audience.

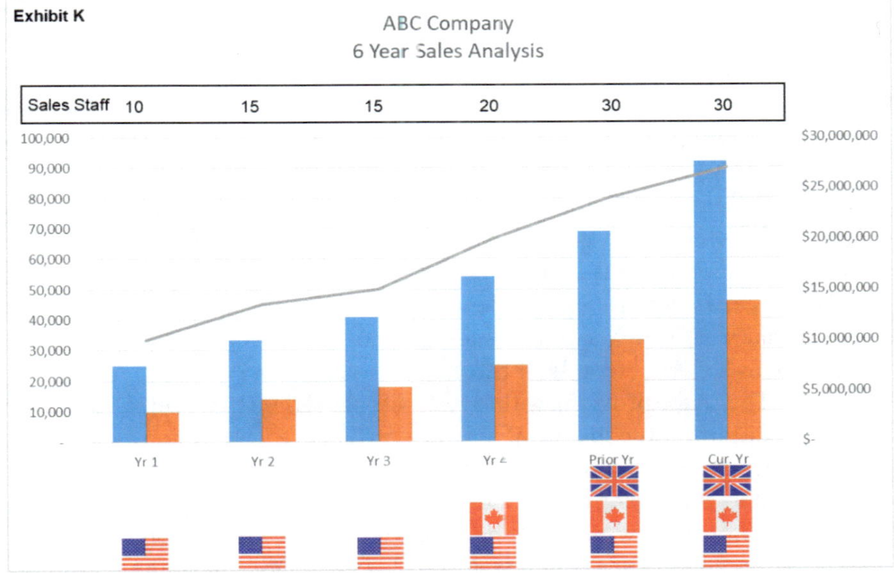

The above chart (Exhibit K) is one example of how this data could be presented. It shows the prospect calls for six years, the corresponding number of sales resulting from those calls, the sales dollars over the six years, the number of sales staff in each of the years, and the number of countries in which the company did business. Other items that could be added include the hit ratio (sales to prospect call ratio), the advertising dollars spent, and changes in staffing, (management, or computer systems).

It is not necessary to label everything. Too many keys and labels add to clutter, not value. The speaker can describe the chart. In our example above, the speaker can explain which axis is used for each graphical element and then give the audience some time to absorb the information.

In summary, every slide should support your main theme, include relevant "Compared to What" and "Why" information, showing results of cause and effect.

Two Ways to Lose Your Audience

Audiences love visual aids because they get more involved in the presentation. They enjoy using their brain and thinking along with the speaker. However, using charts and graphs in a presentation also adds to the risk of losing your audience in two ways: using slides that are overly simple and using slides with good detail, but not giving the audience enough time to fully comprehend them.

Overly simple slides, like those shown in Exhibit A-F, have a single data element without showing any cause-and-effect relationship, show little comparative data (usually just year-to-year comparisons) and do not directly support your main theme. (This discussion of overly simple slides does not include slides that contain a single quote, logo or picture that's sole function is to dramatize the speaker's point). Often, these slides are presented in a rapid-fire manner while the speaker keeps on talking. Here, the speaker has made a first mistake - assuming that people can listen to a speaker while trying to comprehend the parade of slides. Even with the simple slides, the audience needs time to absorb the data before being able to listen again to the speaker. Overly simple slides do not require much time for the audience to absorb, but at least three to five seconds.

The main problem with overly simple slides, however, is that they usually state the obvious, insulting the intelligence of the audience. This causes the speaker to lose credibility. The audience thinks the speaker has misjudged its intelligence level and is presenting too basic a presentation.

When a new slide with detailed relevant data is presented, the speaker should stop speaking for at least 5-10 seconds, depending upon the nature and depth of the slide and the knowledge level of the audience. Five to ten seconds of silence may seem like an eternity when you are standing in front of a group, but your audience needs time to absorb your slide. Take advantage of this time to regroup, gather your thoughts and take a drink of water. Speak when they remake eye contact and are ready to listen again. If all the faces remain glued to the screen, they are not yet ready for you to start again. Wait and watch.

If you do not allow sufficient time to absorb the slide, or if you fail to adequately explain it (regardless of the time displayed), you will notice a "disconnect" with the audience. The audience may be talking amongst themselves trying to determine if they missed something. As a speaker, it is easy to spot the disconnect with the audience - heads moving, small conversations abound and little attention to you. The best real-life example of disconnect I have ever seen was when the speaker showed a slide in the middle of her sentence while continuing to speak. She was stopped by a question and answered it. Upon completing the question, she continued talking and moved onto her next point. The slide remained on the screen for the next ten minutes, but she never referred to it. The audience was abuzz with confusion for the remainder of the talk. At the coffee break, people were saying that the slide looked interesting, asking what it meant and inquiring whether someone could put it back up and explain it to the audience. If the audience was interested in the slide enough to discuss it at the coffee break, is there any doubt it suffered a disconnect.

Using SOS for Charts and Graphs

It is important to get your audience involved in your presentation, even if it is silent participation. One effective technique to increase participation is using SOS (Specific, Overview, Specific). Here's how SOS works: Put a detailed slide up on the screen and allow the audience the usual five to ten seconds to absorb it. Then, say the title of the slide aloud and pick a specific data point. Describe in detail what that specific point signifies. Then, step back and explain the overview concept of the slide. Finally, pick another specific point and describe it in detail. Specific - Overview - Specific. Before moving on, look around the room to make sure all the attendees look like they understand the point. It might be a good time to ask if there are any questions.

Let's look at Exhibit K and see how SOS would work. The speaker may say something like: "Here is the ABC Company's six-year sales analysis. The bar on the far left represents 25,000 prospect calls in year 1. These calls were made by ten sales representatives, in only one country, which resulted in 10,000-unit sales for revenue of $10 million. Overall, you can see the sales trends over a six-year period both in units and dollars. You can also see changes in the number of prospect calls, number of sales staff and number of countries in which we operate. In the current year, we have grown to $28 million in sales, with 46,000-unit sales resulting from 92,000 prospect calls, indicating a hit ratio of 50%. This is up from 40% in 6 years." Notice we went from specific (prospect calls), to overview (six-year trends) to specific (hit ratio).

Pie Charts - They Look Good But...

Pie charts are one of the most often used charts. They are simple and easy to create. They are commonly used to show data such as market share, distribution between business segments, percentage components of an income statement or revenue distribution in various territories. The pie chart is a good way to show a situation at a point in time, but it does not provide much ability to answer the "Compared to What?" question or show cause-and-effect relationship. A pie chart may show, for example, that the company has 40% market share. But we do not know if they are gaining or losing market share, or if they are shifting market share from highly profitable areas to less profitable areas.

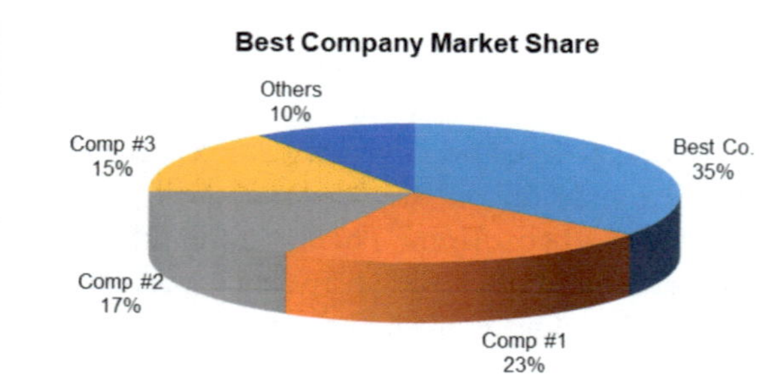

To combat this, some try to use multiple pie charts on the same slide or page. However, graphically, multiple pie charts can be confusing to the eyes.

The audience must bounce from one pie chart to another trying to draw conclusions. If a pie chart is being considered, see whether a different type of chart might work better for your purpose.

Using Flipcharts and Whiteboards

Flipcharts are large pads of paper propped up on an easel. Whiteboards are erasable grease boards you draw on and erase. Both are great for informal presentations for smaller groups. They are ideal for brainstorming sessions or discussion groups. When you are facilitating a group and you need to get an agreement as to direction, you would jot down the ideas generated by the audience and get all the data on the wall in front of them. Some whiteboards are networked and can print the contents of the whiteboard to a printer or email to attendees.

Flip charts have an advantage over whiteboards as you can tear off a sheet from the flip chart and pin it on the wall for later reference. You may have several charts pinned on the wall as you proceed through your presentation. This is amazingly effective especially in brainstorming sessions where one chart may list the pros and another the cons and another the costs and another the budget, etc. Then all the information is spread out on the walls for consideration. Very powerful. However, this does not work well in larger groups or more formal presentations.

Using Models and Props

Besides computer-based slides, flipcharts and whiteboards, the last type of visual aids are Models and Props. Models and props provide the ability for the audience to get a good look at how something will look and operate. It is more engaging than a slide or a flipchart or whiteboard. It is excellent to convey a concept of a future design. A model or prop also creates more credibility because it shows that you have taken more steps than drawing out your ideas on paper, you created some models. Models may be good but may also create confusion as to what the point of the model really is. It might distract from your main point by drawing too much attention to the model itself.

Rules for Presentation Aids

There are basic rules for presentation aids that, if followed, raise your chances of conducting a successful presentation. All of them make it easier for your audience to receive your information. Your slides are intended to support but not obscure your message. Make sure your slides are relevant to your key point and your main theme. Visual aids need to be concise and not confusing. Slides are meant to interpret the data not to present the data. This means that instead of just showing a graph of quarterly sales and gross margins, use the slide to inform the audience what the trend is, where the company is heading and explain the good news or bad news that the data is representing. Do not leave it up to the audience to figure out what to infer from your visual aids.

Use at Least 18 Point Type Face

There are 73 points in an inch. Therefore, 18 point is ¼ inch. If you are putting on a presentation using slides and charts and expect the people in the back of the room to see your words, you must set all type at 18 points or larger. If the audience has to work hard to read your presentation aids, they will not be listening to your words. Exhibit L displays how an 18-point body copy font appears on a slide.

As a rule of thumb, use 28-32 points for heading text and keep your bullet text between 18-28 points. If you use sub bullets you can go as small as 14 points.

Choosing the Right Type Faces

Stay away from
- Times Roman
- Century School Book
- **Wide Latin**
- Book Antiqua
- Bookman Oldstyle

Use
- Arial
- Arial Narrow
- Univers
- **Arial Rounded**
- **Helvetica**

Exhibit L

Avoid Busy Slide Backgrounds

PowerPoint and other presentation programs provide a library of backgrounds to choose from and many of them are very busy. Avoid those. Choose a background that does not obfuscate other information on your slide.

Use High Contrast Colors

User high contrast colors for text and backgrounds and supporting information. And you must avoid using red and green in your slides as 10% of the population has red/green colorblindness and chances are someone in your audience may not be able to understand your presentation if you use red and green throughout.

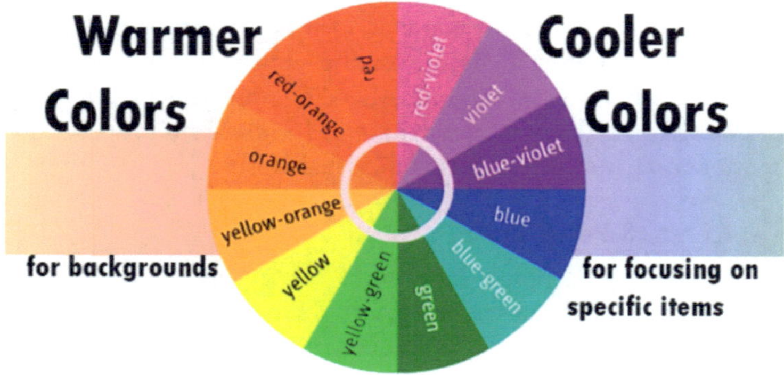

When choosing colors there are some keys to remember. The key is to choose high contrast colors, or colors that are on the opposite side of the color wheel. One common problem presenters find themselves with is using colors that do not have enough contrast making it difficult to read. Warmer colors are great for font colors and specific items, which is the left side of the color wheel. Cooler colors, the right side are generally better for backgrounds. A rule of thumb when choosing colors is that opposite colors provide the best contrast and adjacent colors are good for making subtle differences and effects. If you want to use three colors use a triangle to pick the three colors. Here we see that red, yellow and blue will go well together based on the points of the triangle.

Similarly, if you rotate the triangle, you can find other color combinations that work well together. Keeping in mind that you want the warmer colors as

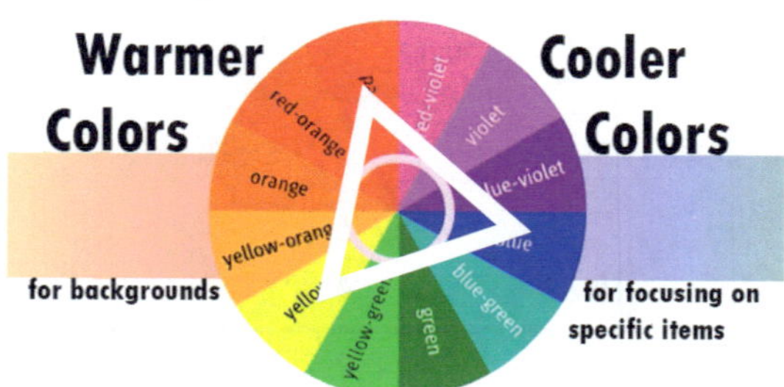

foregrounds, texts and accents, and the cooler colors as backgrounds. However, you can do whatever you want as long as you present a high contrast color scheme, to make sure your slides are readable. It all depends on what you want to accomplish.

Let's take a look at some samples

Orange Text	Orange Text	Orange Text	Orange Text
Or	Or	Or	Or
Red Text	Blue Text	Blue Text	Blue Text
Or	Or	Or	Or
Green Text	Green Text	Green Text	Green Text
Or	Or	Or	Or
White Text	White Text	Red Text	Red Text

Here we see some various background and text combinations. Notice in the first one, the blue background looks good with the orange and red text. The green looks difficult to read since it is closer to blue in color, and the white really stands out. The white always looks great on darker backgrounds. The second one with the red background does not work well with the orange text. The third one with the white background looks good with all the colors chosen but best with the darker colors. And with the yellow background you can see the text color comparisons as well. Your color choices are also based on what you want to accomplish. Here are the psychological color definitions that can assist you with your choices.

While you may think that the colors you choose do not matter, the audience will subconsciously get the hint, even if you are not trying to make one. If you are doing a financial presentation, you probably want to stay away from red since that signifies danger or love or passion. Unless the company is heading into bankruptcy you might want to choose another background color.

Orange Text	Orange Text	Orange Text	Orange Text
Or	Or	Or	Or
Red Text	Blue Text	Blue Text	Blue Text
Or	Or	Or	Or
Green Text	Green Text	Green Text	Green Text
Or	Or	Or	Or
White Text	White Text	Red Text	Red Text

Use San Serif Typefaces

Fonts with tails and feet, called “Serifs, “are tougher to read on an overhead or slide than “San-serif” fonts. Times Roman is an example of a Serif font and Arial is an example of a San-serif font. Again, your goal is to make it easier for the audience to absorb your graphic and verbal presentation. See Exhibit L for samples of serif fonts (stay away from) and san-serif fonts (use).

Avoid Rapid Fire: One Chart After Another

As we saw in Exhibits A-H, it is often better to combine several charts and slides than to have a different chart for each and every piece of data. This is especially true if you have many pieces of information to present. Choose your slides carefully, and use ones that are necessary, comprehensive with multiple data elements and support your main theme. Then give the audience time to absorb each slide. They do not have to understand all of it, but they need to comprehend the basic concept of what it is. If it is a chart, they will look at the axis, the title, the trends of the data points (if they are going up or down), the key (if there is one) and the colors. If it is a slide with bullet points, they generally will read all the points first, and then want to hear you explain them. Similarly, if it is a picture, cartoon or quote they will read it and wait to hear your explanation. Your audience may be able to handle 50 slides in one hour if there are several logos, quotes and basic graphics that only take a few seconds to comprehend. But if you are giving a detailed financial or business presentation and you plan to use dozens of financial charts and graphs, you will likely lose the audience. As information rapidly comes and goes, they will get into the mindset of “Here comes another one!” and lose interest. Use charts and graphs sparingly - this will increase their value to the audience. You don't want to simply narrate a slide presentation. The slides must support the speaker not the other way around.

Avoid Too Much Clipart

Pictures add a dimension to your presentation and clipart can add an entertainment element. However, using too much clipart clutters and detracts from your presentation. Use it sparingly for levity, if at all. You will have much more success focusing your efforts on developing a common theme and using informative charts and graphs to support that theme.

Avoid Keys on Charts

Keys on charts and graphs are necessary when reports are in print and there is no narrator to provide explanations. A key may also be required for charts with large amounts of data. Even when a key is used in a presentation, however, it should be used as a supplement, not a requirement, to understanding the chart. You want your audience to look at the chart and be able to understand it without having to decipher the legend, color schemes and bar names.

Exhibit K is a simple chart that would require a key if in print, to identify the prospect bar, the unit sales bar and the sales dollars line. But the chart functions fine without keys as a presentation aid. An example of a chart that would require a key would be a map indicating by state the degree of market penetration, where each color represents a different level of market saturation (See Exhibit M and Exhibit N).

Avoid Rainbow Scale

The rainbow scale is when you use many colors or shades in your key without regard to how they relate to each other (see Exhibit M). For viewers to understand how ABC Company is doing in each state they would have to look it up in the key. What is the alternative? By using shading appropriately, the audience will easily perceive that the darker the color, the higher the market share concentration (See Exhibit N). The audience only needs to look at the key once to get the percentages of the market share penetration. This way, the key becomes a supplement and not a requirement to understand the chart. When using shading, make sure the audience can easily tell the difference between your shades.

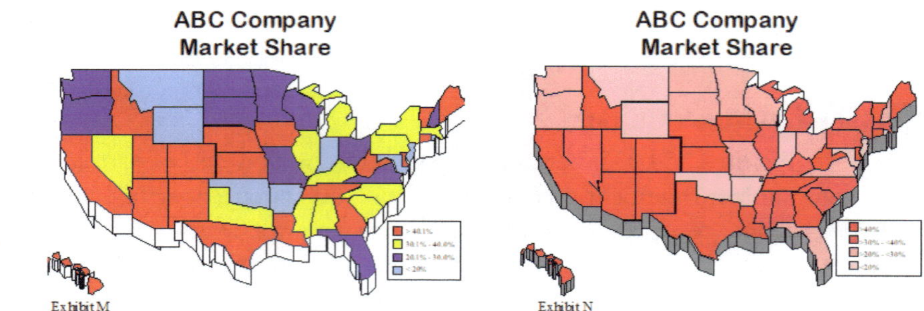

Avoid Dark Backgrounds

Dark backgrounds when used with graphs and charts look good because it makes the details come alive. But, in many facilities, the darker the slide, the darker the room becomes, reducing the presence of the speaker. Also, dark backgrounds with white letters are more difficult to read than dark letters on light backgrounds. If you are looking for every last advantage, use a lighter background.

Avoid Being Automatic

While speakers should maintain eye contact with the audience, they must also pay attention to their visual aids, making sure they are in sync. One speaker I observed would advance a slide and immediately begin speaking about the content of the slide from prepared notes. He did not look at the slides. So, he never noticed that the slide projector advanced two slides on the first click. He was one slide off from his notes for the bulk of the presentation, talking about one set of facts while a different slide was on the screen. Since he faced the audience and often looked down at his notes, he never noticed his miscue. And the audience was too busy being confused trying to figure out the slides, to speak up. The slip was finally caught when the speaker came to a simple slide. Someone finally spoke up and stopped him, but this was 25 minutes into the presentation.

Avoid Typographical and Technical Errors

Nothing can crush your credibility faster than to have slides that are wrought with typographical errors. Spell check can only do so much. Often spell check can assume a word is spelled correctly but not in the context you are using. Have a friend or colleague proofread your slides. Your aids must be technically accurate. Do not show data that supports your position if it is not completely accurate or is misleading. For example, you might say that red cars get more speeding tickets than any other color car. This may or may not be true but leaving out the fact that there are more red cars on the road than any other color, would be a helpful piece of information to help understand the true nature of the issue. With this type of misinformation you might think that you are more likely to get a speeding ticket if you drive a red car, even though that is not necessarily true.

Use Interpretive Slide Titles

Slides are meant to interpret the data not to present the data. This means that instead of just showing a graph of quarterly sales and gross margin, use the slide to inform the audience what the trend is, where the company is heading and explain the good news or bad news that the data is representing. Do not leave it up to the audience to figure out what to infer from your visual aids. For example, many presentations show a financial chart with results for the current and prior year, with the title "Sales – Current and Prior Year," but an interpretive chart title could be "Sales up 20% over Prior Year." This straightaway tells the audience that sales are going up. If you just show the two columns of data, the audience has to work to figure out if sales are up or down and by how much.

The Six Second Rule

How much time do you give your audience to view a visual aid? The general rule is six seconds for charts and graphs, but this time can vary depending on the complexity or simplicity of the individual slide.

Six seconds may sound like a lot, but it is necessary. Even when you have a complicated slide that will be given some explanation, you must give the audience sufficient time to become oriented to it.

This time to absorb is also required for handouts. In fact, you must factor in additional time for the audience to find the correct page. Make sure they get to the correct visual and then give them time to absorb the content.

I once heard a statement that went something like this: "Turn to page six, on the third section, number 4a. The words have been changed to reflect the changes in the law. Now turn to page 8. Number 7c has been deleted, and on page 13, numbers 13-14 have been added to reflect the change in our company policy. On the last page we have changed the words of the following statements."

This was all said with no pauses and no allowances for the audience to catch up. The result was predictable. Everybody was on a different page trying to figure out what was going on, and nobody heard a word of what was being said. Give people time to get to the right page, then begin speaking again. Look at your audience and wait until they all stop turning pages before you begin to talk.

Handouts Versus Slides

Should you use slides or should you use handouts? Many speakers do not like to use handouts because they feel the audience will inevitably be flipping ahead to see what is coming, and not stay focused on the page at issue. The alternative is to hand out the pieces of paper you want the audience to look at one at a time, but that is the wrong way to go because it dramatically slows down the pace of your presentation.

To avoid the paper shuffle, many speakers use slides and promise to give the audience copies at the end of the presentation. Why not distribute the copies in advance of the presentation instead? If you did, the audience would be able to make their notes directly on the handouts, reducing the amount of paper they need to carry home.

The decision to use paper or projections -- or paper and projections -- will depend on each situation. In general, if you are simply reinforcing your main point with a slide and do not expect your audience to retain the specific details of the slide, use a projection on screen. If you want them to study the material and keep it in a file for later reference, hand it out, and provide a link where they can download it.

There is another major factor to consider. The level of detail you are presenting. You can put much more information on a piece of paper than what will be readable on the screen. Trying to make your slides complete and adding more and more elements of information may require that you move to paper. If you feel you have too much information on a chart, but you need it all to make your point, paper is the way to go.

You may want to put several charts on the same page to illustrate that many factors are changing simultaneously. The most common use of this technique is to have separate graphs for each of several key factors all displayed on one page, showing, over time (usually months or years) the current year, current year's plan and last year's actual. Each graph does not have enough meaningful information to stand by itself, but when placed on the same page with other graphs, the audience can look at the total picture on one page and make meaningful comparisons.

Exhibit O

ABC Company – YTD Performance Analysis

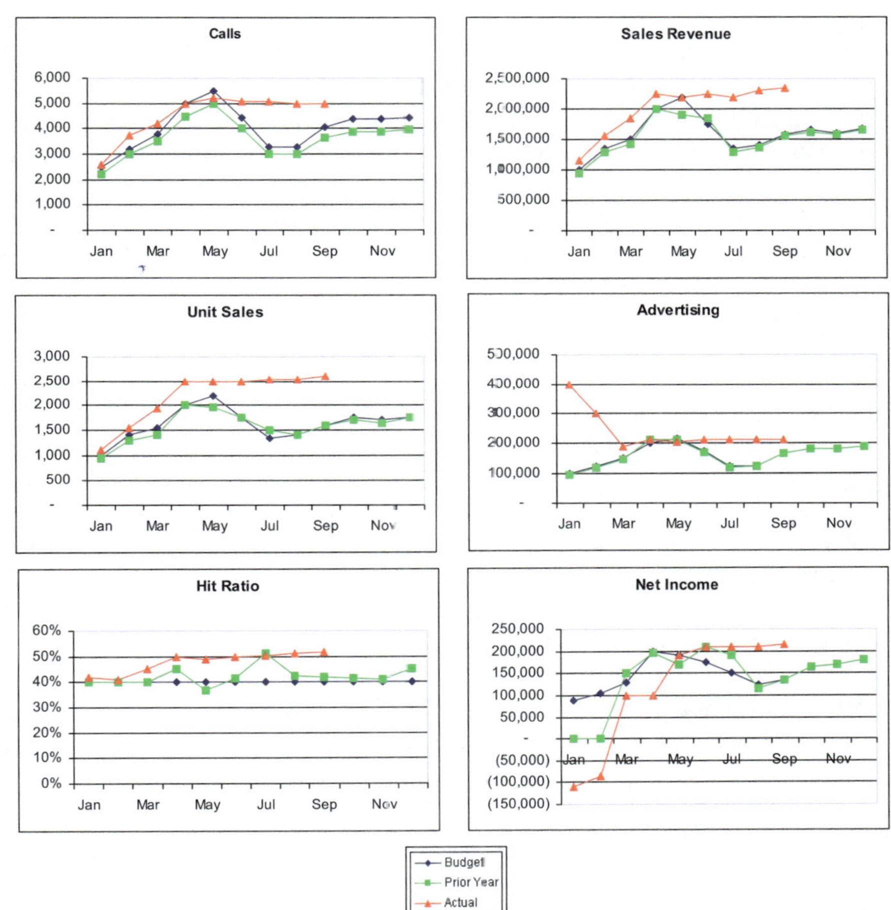

Exhibit O is an example of an effective piece of paper for use during your presentation, versus a single graph that shows only a few of these related elements. Exhibit O shows the relationship between over 200 pieces of data. Data includes six categories, comparing last year, actual year-to-date, and projected year, over 12 months (6 X 3 X 12 = 216). Of course, since the information is only year-to-date through November, we are missing three pieces of data on each graph. But the value of the trending information in a year-to-date fashion can be more valuable now than it will be when the year is complete.

The point of Exhibit O is to allow the audience to study various relationships between categories to see what effect a marketing and advertising blitz has on the bottom line, how a price change has an effect on sales, and how simply increasing the number of calls positively effects the bottom line. There are many things to be learned by the graphs, and by providing this single piece of paper you are accommodating all the learning levels (see discussion of different learning levels in next section). The fast learners are studying relationships beyond the ones you are talking about and drawing their own conclusions. This is what you want. Also, this format allows the audience to see where the company is headed for the rest of the year. If things are looking down at the end of the summer, having last year's data is helpful to show that things will likely turn around in the fourth quarter. Trying to get all this information on a single slide that everyone can understand is impossible.

Your Audience is Participating at 3 Different Levels

Your audience will be comprised of fast learners, slow learners, and others somewhere in between. So, how do you accommodate all these learning levels?

If you try to control the audience and keep them all at the same pace, you will cause the faster learners to get bored. Their minds will start to wander as they wait for the slowest person to get your point. Addressing the fast learners will leave the rest in the dust trying to figure out what is going on. If you address the middle learners, you may have some of the advanced learners getting a little bored, while losing many of the slower learners.

How do you satisfy all of these learning types, and keep them all interested in your presentation? The answer is "handouts" or "links where they can download the handouts." Handouts allow the fast learners to look ahead, the slow learners to look back and the ones in between to remain with you. As the audience refers to their handouts, you may feel that only a small portion of the audience is paying attention. But in actuality, you are addressing the needs of the entire audience. The fast learners can analyze your charts in greater detail or read ahead to see where you are going. The slower learners can flip back and review a few items to better understand your train of thought. (If you use slides, images are removed from the screen and gone forever.) If slower learners can catch up on their own, you will reduce the number of questions you have to stop and answer.

To summarize the pros and cons of using paper versus slides review the following table:

Slides

PROs	**CONs**
• Big and visible, all eyes will be on the screen	• May not accommodate all types of learners
• Simple	• May not be detailed enough to make the point effectively
• Visual effects help reinforce your main point	
• Colorful, can have high impact	• Information is gone when removed from screen, may not address needs of slower learners

Paper

PROs	**CONs**
• Allows speaker to use the detail needed to make point	• Audience will be focused with heads down, not up at the speaker
• Addresses all learner levels	• Speaker may not feel that anyone is paying attention
• High detail will reinforce main point well	
• Allows audience to walk home with something that they can refer to later	• Greater detail takes more skill and time to explain

The Purpose of Bullet Points

Bullet points are meant to be a few words that describe a major point. Yet, too often, bullet points are lengthy sentences that the speaker merely reads to the audience and then moves on.

Bullets should be kept to one line on the slide and comprised of just key words. The speaker is responsible for elaborating on the point that needs to be made. The bullet points are a way for the speaker to outline the points they want to make on a specific topic and allow the audience to see the culmination of thoughts you have comprised on the matter.

Putting a long list of bullet points on the screen as a slide that are detailed in length will require some time before your audience reads them. If you give them the time you will be waiting awhile. You would rather be explaining the points and having the audience listening to you than having them read the bullets in detail, with your narration following.

Here's two examples of a slide showing company goals in bullet points:

Wrong

Current Goals:

1. Hire additional sales staff to facilitate an increase in sales by 20%
2. Implement a price cut of 10% in April to stimulate sales
3. Launch an Advertising Blitz in January and February to increase name recognition
4. Through control of expenses and increase in sales, maintain net income at 10% of sales

Right

Current Goals:

1. Increase calls 20%
2. Price cut of 10%
3. Advertising Blitz
4. Net Income at 10% of Sales

As an audience member, which slide would you rather see? The "Right" way is easy and simple and requires the presenter to explain it. The "Wrong" way is time consuming to read and does not even need a speaker to explain it. What's more, if the speaker does not allow the audience enough time to absorb the content of the slide, whatever explanation is made will probably go unheard.

The bullet point process is simple. Present your slide. Give them a few seconds to absorb it. Then proceed through the bullets one by one.

Often there are two different sets of slides. The sample on the right is used to support the speaker in a live presentation. The longer version of the slides would be used if the speaker is not present. This is common in an investor presentation, when a potential investor asks for your slide deck to review without you being present. In this case, it is better to make sure your bullets are longer, so they stand on their own and have a full description.

Try to limit the number of bullets to no more than 7 on a slide. If you have more than 7 consider using multiple slides or reconsider the point you are trying to make to simply the information being presented.

Progressive Disclosure for Bullet Points

There is some debate on this subject. Whether or not to show all the bullets on a slide at once or use progressive disclosure. It all depends on what you want to accomplish and what you want your audience to focus on. You should avoid using sentences for bullets and use just a few words. This allows you to display the bullet one at a time, the audience can absorb the one bullet in a second and you can elaborate on it more fully. However, if the bullets are longer or displaying them all at once may confuse the audience showing them all at once will require them to spend a few seconds to read them, then refocus on you to explain all of them. For this reason, I believe it is better to use progressive disclosure. This keeps in line with leading them along your magical journey and keeping them on track and altogether.

The debate here is those that believe that the speaker is too controlling or hiding something. The speaker tries to keep the audience glued to one bullet point and restricts participation, particularly among the fast learners. The result is that the speaker may insult the audience with this progressive disclosure or strip-tease method. What can be so important and so secretive that the audience cannot see all the bullets at once? The audience members may feel that they are not trusted to pay attention. Plus, since the audience needs to know where you are going, they cannot tell if there are five points, two points or 10 points to be unveiled. They should be piecing all the informative bullets together as you speak. I use a combination of progressive disclosure and all bullets displayed depending on the slide itself and my objective.

Remember to address the different levels of your audience. And most of all, trust them. Give them the information and explain it as you go. If your message is on target, they will listen.

9. THE SALES PRESENTATION

Sales is the lifeblood of any organization. Without sales, there is no revenue, there is no wages and there is no company. Effective and successful sales come down to presentation. If you are selling products in a grocery store, how the products are presented and laid out on the shelves matters, and if you are selling your products or services to your clients, your sales presentation is the key to success. Nothing can make a prospect forget your company faster than a bad presentation. This is your chance to impress them, knock their socks off, get them to insist upon hiring your company. If you show that you have done your homework on them, demonstrate you understand their business, how they make their money, what differentiates them in the marketplace and what their needs are, you are off to a good start.

Doing Your Homework on Your Prospect

Nothing makes a prospect feel more important and special than when you have taken the time to learn about their company and what they stand for. On the flip side, nothing will turn off a prospect more than trying to jam your one-size-fits-all presentation down their throats without regard for their company and their products. People like to feel special. They like to feel that you went through the effort to find out about them and understand them. Do your research. Read their website, checkout their social media posts, read their blogs. Understand what their mission is and what their competitive advantage is. How long they have been in business? Who are their major clients? Read some of the testimonials. Try to anticipate what issues and problems they may have that your products and services can address.

This knowledge as you demonstrate, will create credibility in you and your company, and they will respect you more and listen more carefully. They will believe that you cared enough about them to do a little research on them, and now you have their attention. If you show that you spent time researching them, they will be more willing to participate in and actively listen to your presentation.

Know Your Products and Services

I know that this sounds obvious, but you really need to be an expert on the products your company offers. It's not good enough to just know what they are, you need to understand how they work, what issues you have had, the history and evolution of the products, which major companies are using them and how they have benefited from them. You must be the expert about your products and services. You must assume your prospect has never heard of you, your company or your products and be prepared for that. Do not act surprised if they never heard of you.

The company history is important. Some companies will not do business with companies that have not been in business for at least 3 to 5 years. Know why your company was founded, what the progression and growth has been, and more importantly, what the core values and mission of the Company are.

Does your company have any history with this prospect? If yes, you need to research what that history is. Did it end badly? What were the issues? Have they been corrected?

Learn about your prospect's market and their industry they operate in. Is the market growing? Is it flooded with competition? Try to envision how your products and services can help them exceed their goals in their own marketplace.

Know who you are competing against for this business. Identify your strengths and weaknesses against the competition and prepare to address this in your presentation. You never want to trash the competition, but merely point out some of the advantages your product has over the competition.

Customizing Your Company's Standard Pitch

Every organization should have a standard sales presentation, but that sales presentation is not a one-size-fits-all approach. It is just a starting point. The first thing to customizing your sales pitch is to cut the fat from the presentation. If you have a long list of products or services, remove the items that do not belong. Only include information that is relevant to the prospect. You do not want your prospect thinking "Gee, that's great but we do not have a need for that." If your research was done adequately in your preparation, you will have a good idea what stays and what goes. Your presentation needs to focus on your prospect's needs and wants and how you are going to solve their problems.

Now that you know the issues your prospect may be facing, and which products and services can help them solve these problems, make the connection with the benefits you offer with those needed solutions. This is where you demonstrate to them how your product will reduce costs, increase sales, enhance customer service, or improve employee productivity and how the prospect will be more efficient and ultimately more profitable for using your solution. Here is where you can highlight the reasons why your product is superior to the competition and use verifiable statistics if you have them available.

A simple thing to make a connection with your prospect is to include their logo throughout your presentation.

Include Case Studies and Testimonials

People are naturally herd animals and have resistance to going it alone. They do not like to venture out where no one has gone before. To that end, providing case studies and testimonials of others that have had good experiences with your products and services can ease the "go it alone" fear. If you do not have testimonials, call your happy clients, and get some.

Presentation Leave Behinds

While most sales are not inked on the first sales presentation, there is a period of time after you have delivered your presentation and answered all the questions and addressed all the objections, that needs a little something. Otherwise, just walking out is awkward. This is the ideal time to break out your leave behinds. This does not have to be anything extravagant but something to remember you. It should be professional, meaning professionally printed on heavy stock, semi-gloss paper, bleeding edges and include images. Also consider leaving behind some small promotional item, like a pen with your company name and logo on it. The goal is to keep you in their thoughts and seeing your name on a pen every time they use it will register in their brains. Caution: The cost between a quality pen and a cheap pen is about $0.15 each for 500. You do not want to give them a cheap pen that breaks and they throw out right after they look at your company name and logo.

If you walk out without leaving anything, that is awkward. If you leave a copy of your slides, that is unprofessional, unless of course they ask for them. Maybe there were some statistics and comparisons on the slides that interested them, and they wanted to take a closer look. I would be a little hesitant about giving them your entire slide deck but ask which pieces of information they want and then email them when you get back to the office. It gives you a reason to reconnect with them too.

Sales Presentation Structure

The structure of your sales presentation is straight forward, but it is crucial to get it right. Your introduction will include the Prospects Needs or the problem they need you to solve, how your specific products and services will benefit the prospect so they can make an immediate connection. Also include who you are, what your company is, some background on both and why you are here today. Include a timeline of when the product will be delivered, or solution will be completed and keep all your statements and promises realistic. There is never a good time to over promise.

Sales Presentation Body

In the body of your presentation, you cover the details of the products and services to be provided that will directly impact the operations of the prospect company. Provide enough detail to get them interested and to make the connection. Do not go overboard with detail, it will confuse them, and you will lose them. If you do not provide enough detail, they will not make the connection on why they should purchase from you at all.

Include any verifiable statistics in the body to support your recommended solution. What do you foresee as the estimated cost savings and how you came up with that number? Was there some increased productivity to be realized? Show how you calculated that number. Other statistics to show include reduced defects, lower returns, less customer support issues, faster turnaround times, increased throughput etc. Also in the body is the time for explaining the cost of your products or services. The level of detail to provide here depends on how complicated your solution is. If you are simply providing a product and installing it, show those two items. If you are performing services to streamline the production line with multiple products and studies etc. you need to provide some more detail on a task-by-task basis.

Closing Your Sales Presentation

If you have done a good job in the introduction and the body, the prospect should be ready for your presentation close. This is your last chance and you must convince them. Summarize the benefits to the client showing cost savings, enhanced customer support, increased sales, or increased employee productivity. This is the time to ask for the call to action, which could be the next step in the approval process. Depending on the type of product or service you may even ask for a credit card or a signed purchase order, but typically there will be some deliberation and follow up before the deal closes.

Delivering a Sales Presentation

Making a sales presentation to a prospect is different than making a presentation to an audience. When you get a chance to make a sales presentation to a prospect, chances are there was considerable work done beforehand to get that opportunity. Something they learned about you and your company led them to give you this opportunity. So often when people get this one chance to make the pitch, they send in their most polished professional, well-rehearsed salesperson, the one that knows the standard presentation and list of product features and provides some entertaining anecdotes and stories. But that is not what the prospect wants. Do they really want to take time out of their day to hear about your exhaustive list of products, your company history, the founder, how many locations you have, your growth in revenue, etc.? No. If you run through a list of boring prepared slides of features and benefits, they may start looking to the exit.

Never, never, never present the same presentation to every customer without regard to size, industry, geography, or other specific problems of the prospect.

You must make them feel different and special. If you are running the same presentation, it will be obvious to them, and you will not make a connection.

If you get a chance to pitch them and you underperform, the prospect will immediately think your products will underperform as well.

Remember these Sales Presentation Guidelines:

1. **Remember Your Customer** – This is all about your customer and their needs and how you are going to solve their problems. It is not about you.

2. **Be Focused and Direct** - Focus on your main points and get to them quickly. Do not meander your words and get off track. Stay on point.

3. **Demonstrate Flexibility** - Show them that your company is flexible and focused on their needs. You must convey that you are creative and prepared and willing to work with them to get them exactly what they want and that you will go the extra mile for them.

4. **Ask Questions** – the best way to make your prospect feel like they are part of the solution is to ask them questions. You did your research and anticipated what some of the issues are, and you demonstrated your knowledge of their company and their market, which will allow them to open up to you with their real issues. You cannot provide the right solution if you do not know their exact needs. A good sales presentation is much more of a discussion than just a salesperson flipping through a litany of slides.

5. **Tell Stories** – The best way to connect with the people in the room is to tell stories. Tell stories they can relate to. This will also show how much you know about their business, too. Try to connect with each person at some level. When you talk, look straight in the eyes of each person for a few seconds. Ask rhetorical questions to get them thinking. Stories that make them

laugh or off-the-cuff instant humor helps create that connection too. Instead of droning on about your products and services, talk about how your company's products and services have helped other companies overcome their obstacles and become successful.

6. **Take Notes** – when the prospect answers your questions, take notes. It makes them feel that what they are telling you is important to you and is going to make a difference in getting the right solution at the right price.

7. **Show Enthusiasm and Energy** – If you are not excited about your solution, do not expect them to get excited about you either. People love to help others and if you demonstrate a true enthusiasm about solving their problem, it will show and go a long way in establishing credibility and trust.

8. **Believe in Your Solution** – Going hand-in-hand with enthusiasm is to believe in your products and the solution you are presenting. Intertwining the benefits of the product with the needs of the prospect marries the two and creates a bond that will move the sale forward.

9. **Be Genuine and Consistent** – Honesty is key. Be authentic and do not try to fake anything. Make sure your attitude, your actions and your words are all saying the same thing. 80% of communication is nonverbal so your words may be saying one thing and your body another.

10. **Use a Flipchart or Whiteboard** – A flipchart or whiteboard is extremely effective in connecting the prospects problems to the solutions you propose, especially when you are drawing out their process that needs to be fixed and drawing in your solution. It is immensely powerful. When you discuss key figures and points, add them to the diagram, so they stay visible throughout the discussion.

These guidelines help to make the connection with your prospect, and makes people want to do business with you. If you do these things, you will be likeable, you will appear competent, caring and sincere, and they will want to do business with you.

Looking and Presenting Professionally

Appearance and professionalism play deciding roles in many sales presentations, especially if the quality and type of services do not differ significantly among competitors. For example, suppose two large accounting firms are competing for a new client. One major accounting firm can probably perform its primary services just as well as another. The small service differences may not be a factor in the client selecting the accounting firm. So how does the client decide which firm to choose? Simple! They choose the one that makes the best impression. The one that appeals to them more. In other words, they choose the one that makes an emotional connection with them. This can be done by connecting on a personal level, sharing stories of similar clients in the same industry, or just relating better. An emotional connection can also be conveyed if it has better looking materials, a more sophisticated presentation, and a smoother more confident presenter. The client rationalizes that the firm that looks better, is more organized, is skilled at presentations and takes advantage of state-of-the-art technology will be more skilled in the handling of accounting matters. It may not be true but looks do count for a lot. Or maybe their children play on the same little league team and the connection was made at that level. Don't leave emotional connections at the door.

Today, being high-tech in your presentations counts for a lot. Using state-of-the-art presentation aids, such as computer-generated graphics and well-designed handout materials, will help sell your message, product or service. Using the latest tools to aid your presentation will convey to your prospect that you and your company are progressive. If handouts are to be provided, always provide a link on the internet where the audience can download the electronic version at their convenience and if the group is not too large, consider handing out a flash drive with all the materials on it.

If your presentation is outdated, prospects will assume that your products may not be state-of-the-art either. For example, an insurance company that still requires clients to complete paper applications may be inferred to be using antiquated paper intensive systems and not structured to take advantage of high technology to reduce processing costs. Hence, they may be perceived to be passing the cost of inefficiency on to their policyholders through higher premiums.

Speed in delivery of follow-up materials and answers to client questions is also a sign of a company taking advantage of high technology. Through efficient business processes and computerization, our example insurance company can process the application and return a quote within hours, compared to paper-intensive operations which may take a week to process a quote. This will make a positive impression, and these positive impressions are what make the difference.

10. WORKING WITH EQUIPMENT

It is pretty easy to jot down in your notes to present this slide here and demonstrate this item there. But if it is not practiced with the actual equipment, the risk of failure increases. Some high-tech equipment, although easy to use once mastered, takes time to learn. Make sure you know how to turn it on, plug it in, connect it to your computer, and adjust the colors, brightness, and focus.

The Two Step Shuffle

It is equally important to make sure your equipment works in the room you will be doing your presentation. You do not want to be shuffling back and forth between where you need to stand to advance to the next slide and where you need to stand to be out of the way so the audience can appropriately view the slide. Map out a place to stand and speak and be relatively close to where you need to be to control your visual aids. Learn to use a remote control to advance your presentation slides to minimize the need to be close to the computer, but test and make sure the remote is working properly beforehand.

Using a Microphone to Assure Being Heard

We mentioned before the importance of speaking loudly and with authority. When necessary, use a microphone. There is nothing more frustrating to an audience member than trying to listen intently but only receiving bits and pieces of the intended message. Test the microphone beforehand. Handheld microphones have different levels of sensitivity – some require you speak closely to the microphone while others do not. Make sure the speakers are of high quality to project your voice the tonal quality you require.

Working With a Pointer

Pointers are usually used when a chart or illustration has too many elements on it and the speaker needs to highlight a specific area that he or she cannot guide the audience to with words. This is often a sign that the slide needs to be simplified. However, there are instances when a pointer is appropriate.

For example, if the slide is showing a product life cycle, the speaker will point to a particular spot on the curve and then proceed to discuss the phase of the cycle.

The pointer should be used to point once to the object, leaving it in place for up to five seconds to allow the audience to focus there. Then remove it.

Using pointers are okay, but there are some things to watch out for. Do not:

- Move the pointer onto and away from your spot without giving your audience time to tune into where you are pointing
- Keep the pointer on the spot for an extended period of time, because it will distract your audience
- Use a pointer just for the sake of pointing
- Use a laser pointer to activate objects on the screen of a computer when a smoother operation could be accomplished with either a mouse or keyboard stroke
- Use a laser pointer if you are not familiar with it.

Timing is Everything

To be effective as a speaker you have to work well with your equipment and be in sync with its performance. You need to operate crisply and without glitches. Visual aids supporting your points should appear when you need them.

Equipment (Online, Overhead and Slides)

Here are some common things to keep in mind to ensure a smooth performance with audio-visual equipment:

1. Keep out of the way so the audience can see the image
2. Speak to the audience, not to the slide
3. Adjust the lights for the best effect
4. Learn how to troubleshoot the equipment in case something goes wrong (lightbulb, focus, on/off switch, etc.)

11. TECHNIQUES TO MITIGATE STAGE FRIGHT

Anytime you do something you are not familiar with, you will experience a little trepidation because of the unknown. If you attempt to ski down a black diamond run for the first time you will feel fear and hesitancy, but the more you do it the more confident you become and the easier it gets, and the fear factor lessens. You may still get that exhilaration of swooshing down the slopes, but the fear of death will wane over time.

Signs of Stage Fright

You will be standing in front of an audience you may or may not know. You are not sure how they will receive you. Will the equipment work? Will the microphone work? Will you have a frog in your throat? Do they really want to hear what you have to say? All these questions and more are racing around in your head. This makes you nervous and anxious. Your heart may be pounding irregularly. You might have difficulty concentrating or focusing on your material. Your legs may get wobbly and you might feel dizzy. Or worse, you have a dry and constricted throat. It is very identifiable in speakers as their voices will sound higher pitched than normal. You may even get nauseous or experience sweaty palms. If you experience any of these, you are experiencing stage fright. First, you must identify it, then you have to incorporate a strategy to alleviate it.

Spiraling Progression of Stage Fright

How does stage fright manifest itself into your presentation? It progresses through 4 phases, and each stage enables more panic in the next phase. The first phase is what is going on in your head before the presentation even starts. It is the anticipation of a negative outcome. You may feel that you are not as prepared as you want to be and worry about performing badly because of poor preparation. You may worry that you created your presentation at a level that is not commensurate with the education level of the audience. You could be either talking over their heads or boring them with trivial stuff they already know. If you do not know who is in your audience, this could be scary.

Now that you predicted failure and got yourself worked up, the second phase is how you respond to that prediction. If you feel something will go wrong and there is nothing you think you can do about it, this will create a higher degree of anxiety. You first predict you are going to fail, so you start to worry about failing, and that will create a dry throat, a pounding heart, nauseousness, and other physiological effects on your body. If you just felt confident that things would go well, you could simply have avoided all these symptoms.

The next phase happens when you are doing your presentation. Assume, your presentation is going along smoothly. The audience is loving it and you are proceeding on schedule. Then, you start to check your anxiety levels. Your focus shifts to wondering about what the audience is really thinking. You notice one person checking their phone and you wonder if you are boring them. Then another gets up to use the bathroom. You start to think, were they frustrated with you? Your attention is shifted away from delivering an awesome presentation to worrying about your audience. As a result, your delivery and your presentation suffer. The quality declines. At this point you start making mistakes in your presentation and leave certain information out altogether. Making mistakes causes you to reassess your level of anxiety more and then forces you to focus even more on the failures of your presentation creating a further downward spiral of your presentation. At this point, some presenters may cut their presentation short and walk off the stage. An excessive amount of anxiety will cause a speaker to lose their place and forget what they were going to say, and ultimately end their presentation abruptly. But it does not have to be that way.

Techniques to Overcome Stage Fright

"Only the prepared speaker deserves to be confident."
– Dale Carnegie

There are 5 main things you can do to help you manage the stress caused by stage fright. The most important one is the first one – preparation. If you are totally prepared, know your material inside and out, did an awesome job creating your visual aids and have prepared for questions, you should be confident and have no fear. Sounds simple right? Well, it's not that simple. That is only the first step.

If you are nervous you need to do some relaxation exercises and some visualization to calm your nerves. First, before your presentation do some exercising. This can be running, walking, or going to the gym. It does not have to be major, just something that gets your blood flowing and gets your lungs processing air. When you exercise and breathe heavier than normal you expel some of those future throat clearing gremlins. In addition to raising your breathing, do some vocal cord exercises by practicing speaking loudly and doing some humming. You do not want to go on stage and find out you have not even spoken to anyone yet, only to spend a minute to clear your throat. I have a few pages of tongue twisters I recite out loud before I make any presentation.

Next do some muscle release drills. Sit in a chair and concentrate on flexing different muscles and then releasing them. I typically start with the calf's and work my way up to the thighs, abdomen and then the arms, neck, and shoulders. Roll your head and relax your neck. Try to feel like you are in complete control of your body. This might sound silly but stick your tongue out as far as it goes to stretch it.

The last thing to do in this category is to use visualization or imagery. Imagine yourself in front of the audience delivering the perfect presentation where the audience is totally engaged and think you are a rock star. These techniques should help you to prepare for your presentation and should reduce most of your anxiety associated with stage fright.

Now that you are relaxed you are ready to change your perspective. This is especially doable right after you imagined yourself successfully presenting in the previous step. You have been selected as the expert to give a presentation on a specific topic. Remember that. They selected you because you have knowledge or information that the audience needs. Not only that, but they believe you are the best person to delivery this information. Think about that and it should dispel your fear. Additionally, you should modify your behavior in front of the audience. Instead of being glued rigidly to the podium, see if you can move around the room. Go up and down the aisle talking if you can, and it works with your presentation. Moving relaxes the mind and makes you feel more in control of the entire room. Also, make sure you include some stories and anecdotes if they are relevant. When people tell stories instead of reciting prepared words, they become more natural and more confident in their delivery. Then when you get back to your slides you will be more comfortable and relaxed.

Finally remember who you are. You are a collection of your experiences, education, and knowledge. They came to hear you, the natural you, the human you. Be yourself, and you'll do great. Even if you do make a few missteps in your presentation the audience knows you are human and will appreciate you being comfortable enough to be yourself in front of them.

12. DEALING WITH QUESTIONS

When you have the attitude that you are going to conquer your audience with your presentation, your presentation is more likely to be fun. But dealing with unanticipated questions and objections can change your fun into panic. No matter how hard you prepare and how many key points and supporting information you include in your presentation, there will be questions.

Setting the Ground Rules for Questions

It is a good idea to set the ground rules for questions at the beginning of your presentation. If you are conducting a small group brainstorming or strategy session you want to encourage your audience to feel free to ask questions at any time. This can be risky for most presentations and especially so for larger groups, as the flurry of questions could derail your presentation regarding your timeline. To be cognizant of the time constraints it is always better to defer questions to a specific time, typically the end of the presentation. When you are planning your presentation and if you have been allocated an hour you may plan on 45 minutes for your presentation and 15 minutes for questions, but if you open it up throughout the presentation there is no way to make sure you will stay on track. Ideally, tell the audience up front that you have reserved time at the end for questions, and please save their questions until then. If your presentation is informative and leading the audience through a magical journey, their questions will probably be answered later in your presentation. That would be a good reason to defer questions to the end of the presentation. For longer presentations or presentations that cover a myriad of topics, you may want to stop at the end of each topic and ask if there are any questions about the topic you just finished. If you wait until the end for all questions for all topics, it might be too overwhelming for you and the audience.

Preparing for Questions

As part of your preparation you have researched your audience and researched your topic and included the relevant information in your presentation to effectively get your point across. But with 3 different types of learners, distractions like smartphones and conflicting interpretations, there will be questions for you. Understand your audience and try to anticipate the types of questions they may ask. If you are presenting to upper management, be prepared to explain the financial impact of everything you are talking about. How much will it cost, how much will it drive revenues, etc.? Whereas if you are making a presentation on creating

Microsoft Office presentations, be prepared to get questions about format and layout and other technical tricks.

Try to think a little outside the box to anticipate those obscure questions that are not so obvious. If you are making a presentation about a new streamlined manufacturing floor process, you might get a question that asks if it would be cheaper to acquire another company that already has that process in place. It is difficult to prepare for some of these questions, but they will come. Remain calm and mention that you will check into it and get back to them.

To minimize the risk of getting ambushed by a question you have difficulty answering, prepare a list of potential questions ahead of time, while you are preparing your presentation. This will allow you to structure your answers so if these questions do come up, you have a confident ready-made answer handy. If you practice your presentation in front of a friend or colleague, have them help you with some sample questions.

How to Ask for Questions

When it is time to ask them for questions, how should you ask for them? Don't say "Does anyone have any questions." That is too broad. There is a restaurant in San Jose California that if the waiter or waitress asks you "How is everything" you get your meal for free. The rationale is that it is not personal and specific enough. The waiter or waitress is supposed to ask, "How was that turkey club" and make it personal. "Did you get enough chips with that?" That creates a real connection with the customer. And when a waiter asks a broad question, they tend to get a non-response, like "fine." The same thing applies with your presentation. If you ask too broad a question you might not get any. If you must, lead them to ask questions about a specific issue. "We discussed the tax implications of moving our operations to a low tax state, does anyone have any questions about that?" You have a lot better chance of getting some questions with this approach.

Handling Questions

Here are some guidelines on how to handle the questions and answers.

1. **Maintain your persona.** Do not be confident and bold during the presentation and meek and mousy during the Q&A session. Keep the same personality, the same style, the same stature, and the same tone of voice.

2. **Repeat the question.** For the benefit of the audience repeat the question, so they all can hear. This will also give you time to formulate an answer.

3. **Acknowledge a good question.** They say there are no bad questions, but that is not true. Acknowledge when you get a good question, one that is thought-provoking and demonstrates that they listened to your presentation. Do not acknowledge every question as a good question as that devalues the compliment.

4. **Be brief, but not too brief.** Do not answer with a one-word answer like Yes or No, but do not give a long-winded answer when a short one will do.

5. **Address the questioner**. When a question is asked look directly at the person that asked the question. Also, walk towards the person to show your interest and maintain your status of being in control. If you move backwards away from the questioner, it might show a sign of weakness. As you answer the question look into the eyes of the person that asked it but move to the other side of the room looking for the next question after you complete your answer. Look away after answering. If you are looking right at the person that asked the question when you finish it sends a signal to them to ask a follow up question. Follow up questions are not bad, but they will feel less able to launch that follow up if you pick on another audience member from a different part of the room.

6. **Admit not knowing an answer.** If you get a question that you do not know the answer to, admit it. You cannot make up something that may prove to be wrong. You are only human and do not have all the answers at your fingertips.

7. **Acknowledge over questioners.** You will get over questioners in your audience. These are people that like to hear themselves talk so they ask repeated questions and keep asking. You cannot let your Q&A turn into a two-person discussion. Acknowledge their issues and ask to speak to them after the session is over.

8. **Acknowledge soap box questions.** There may be some people that get up to speak on their soap box about some issue. They may disagree with your message and provide their opinion on how the issue should be handled but they don't ask a question, they just opine. Thank them and move on to the next question. You don't want to get into a debate as that is a no-win situation.

9. **Prepare for difficult questioners.** There are some people that just like to be difficult. They will ask questions that may make no logical sense, but they ask it anyway which may be intended to trip you up. They can also ask questions that contradict an earlier question that they themselves asked. I remember one situation where an audience member stood up to ask a question about why we were not including foreign currencies in the ERP system, even though we were a domestic company. When we explained that all reporting was done in local dollars and any sales transactions on the web were converted at the time of purchase there was no need to keep the foreign currencies in the accounting system. This person then suggested that we were wrong to allow people to purchase online using different foreign currencies. Huh? They just contradicted their own argument. In a case like this, move on to the next question.

10. **Expect to be haggled.** Expect to be interrupted by someone that does not like your answer. Luckily, if you have a microphone, you have the louder voice. Handle the interrupters like the over questioners – ask them to talk to you after the session.

11. **What if no questions?** The last issue is what if you don't get any questions. It happens. It could be that you were the last speaker in a long line of speakers and the audience wants to get out, or you covered your material so well there truly are no questions. In this case, you should prepare some expected questions and ask the audience if they had one of your prepared questions. If still no, then restate your main theme, your key points and ask for a call to action.

Body Positioning for Questions

The most eloquent presentation may be stymied by poor handling of questions. However, if you take your time and prepare your answers carefully, you will be fine. The mere fact that someone challenges or questions your statements can be intimidating. And whether you realize it or not, your body language may get defensive.

Defensive posture should be avoided at all costs. Do not fold your arms across your chest or touch your face with your hands. Most important, never back up. This, in essence, is retreating, a sign of lack of confidence and vulnerability.

Instead, as the person asks a question or poses an objection, you should move toward them. This signals that you are taking the issue head on and are confident that you can answer it effectively. When the question is completed, continue to move toward the questioner as you begin your answer. Look directly at the person who asked the question, then continue responding but move your attention to the other side of the room. This will include the entire audience in the answer.

When you have completed your answer look anywhere but at the person who asked it. This is a signal that you are ready for another question. If you finish looking at the person you started with, the audience may feel that you are carrying on a one-on-one conversation with this person. Also, the person may feel obligated to follow up and ask another question.

"Any Questions" Count to 10

When asking whether there are any questions, many speakers look quickly around the room and proceed. They look up for a couple of seconds, put their head down and continue. To get all the questions, you should count to ten, while looking around the room for hands. This will indicate to your audience that you really want to field questions, and that you do respect their input. Anything less than ten seconds is too short.

Allow Yourself Time to Think...

Thinking on your feet while fielding questions in front of a large group is tough. So, build in some time to think about your answers. Some people repeat the question; others restate it. Either way, they are simply allowing themselves time to formulate an answer.

Listen to the entire question, before beginning to respond. After you hear it, you may want to restate it to allow the audience to hear it, and after that, use a short pause.

...Then Get to the Point

Once you have accumulated your thoughts be precise, and quick with your answer. State your position and then back it up with an explanation of why you feel that way. Done! Do not talk and talk about a random collection of thoughts. You need to be precise. Identify what the question is. Zero in and answer it.

Treat each response to a question like its own mini presentation. Use an introduction (state your point or opinion), support it (why you believe it) and then state your conclusion.

Do Not Filibuster

Filibustering is speaking without really saying anything: not making a point, not leading the audience anywhere, and sometimes not even making sense. The only people that intend to filibuster are politicians, but some speakers do it without even realizing it. When a question arises, they begin to respond with whatever comes out of their mouth.

Often filibuster responses include dragging up the past, referring to things that did not work and pointing out why they probably will not work in the future. When people are addressing current and future problems, nobody likes to be dragged back into the mud of previous failures.

For example, suppose a question is raised about how the new system will handle the processing of product returns. A filibuster response would refer to the old system and go on and on about how bad it was at handling returns, and what a difficult system it was to use. Why is this person bringing up the old system? It only acts to lower the enthusiasm in the room. To keep momentum alive, you may quickly acknowledge that the old system had faults and point out that is why we are making sure the new system can process returns effectively. No mud, no old complaints, and no loss of momentum. Be precise, be positive and people will appreciate you for it.

Avoid Bear Trap Questions

When soliciting feedback, be careful not to alienate your audience by asking bear trap questions. Bear trap questions are ones that have your point of view buried within them. "Don't you agree we should change our marketing plan for next year?" is a bear trap question. If anybody in the room does not think that the company should change its marketing plan, the speaker has just alienated them and trap them into either agreeing with the statement or raising conflict. They will now be tougher to win to your side.

You could ask, "What do you think we need to do in the area of marketing for next year?" as a more open-ended question. But this question may be a little too open if you are addressing the marketing planning committee. Here, if your goal is to change the marketing plan, start with something apt to stimulate a knowledgeable discussion. You could say, "What are the three most important elements of our marketing plan for next year and why are they crucial for our success?" This question will allow the group to vocalize their most important items. From their responses you can tell what areas can and cannot be changed. After getting the "must haves" identified, ask them to identify other areas that may be altered to provide a better or more focused approach. This undoubtedly will generate comments. Without suggesting that the marketing plan be changed, you have successfully identified the areas that need to be changed and generated "buy-in" from the committee.

Always Start With What You "Can Do"

People like to hear solutions rather than problems. The most productive meeting I have ever attended started with a ground rule that no one could say the word "can't." And if anyone presented a problem, they needed to provide at least one solution to it.

The least productive meetings I have attended are those where members of a group simply attack a proposal without offering any alternative solution. They will only provide reasons why something new will not work. The one person trying to keep things upbeat presents an alternative solution, incorporating the nay-sayers concerns, but it is batted down again as the nay-sayers identify more reasons why that will not work either. When asked for a solution, a typical nay-sayer response may be, "It's not my job, all I know is we can't!"

You cannot easily change the attitudes of these nay-sayers. Just keep positive and solutions oriented. Maybe it will rub off on the rest of the group.

13. PRESENTATIONS FOR EXPERTS

It is quite common for people that obtained success to be asked to give a presentation. Often this is the case when somebody becomes successful launching a start-up company or has lost a lot of weight or has gained some notoriety. The groups that attract these presenters have audiences that want to hear the speaker and learn something. They do not necessarily want to hear someone talk about their successes as much as they want to hear a plan that they can execute to become successful too. It's a very fine line. Very few people obtain success entirely on their own. I believe the worst presentation I ever saw, was a guy that set up this enormous company, and he essentially said he did it all himself. At the end of his presentation, I don't think anyone in the audience believed him. What people want to hear are some pitfalls, challenges, and setbacks that they incurred on their journey, so people can relate more and understand that it is not easy. In contrast to the above example, the better presentation would be one that lays out the ingredients that one must do to be successful. While no one believed that this one guy could do it on his own, it is refreshing to the audience when people admit they cannot do it all themselves.

For example, the technology startup company needs to have at least three full time dedicated resources, one dedicated sales and marketing, one dedicated to managing technological development and another to oversee the operations, finance and accounting. No one person can do it all and standing up in front of the audience telling them that you did it all is simply not believable.

The audience will be interested in your presentation if you can guide them through your personal journey so they can follow it and can use it as a roadmap to be successful too. Often there is luck and chance and various other variables come into play but having a roadmap they can walk away with after a presentation will be invaluable to your audience.

14. OTHER TYPES OF PRESENTATIONS

The previous sections of this book focused on developing in-depth business presentations using slides and running in length up to a couple hours or more. The techniques outlined in this book apply to other types of presentations as well. You may not realize it, but we make presentations every day, some just casual conversations, some slightly more formal. We should always frame our perspective in a way that paints a picture or tells a story to create interest and requires follow up from your audience. You might be walking down the hall and bump into a colleague who asks you if you made a decision on the impasse you are facing on the project you have been working. I am not talking about a full fledge prepared story line, but you should start with some interesting facts about the project, trying to pique his interest and garner that "Tell me more" response from him. Then move along with your story to explain the options, and then close with how you made your decision. For example, you had an issue with the technology for logging on the storefront, and the vendor with the best solution was twice the price of the competitors, but that would have blown the budget. We negotiated the price down and got the solution we were looking for and stayed within our budget.

Other presentations can be a little more formal, but still relatively brief.

The Elevator Pitch

"You only have one chance to make a first impression."

An elevator pitch is a 30-second introduction of yourself, a product, a service or a company, where the objective is to get the person or group listening to want to hear more and ultimate hire you. The term "Elevator Pitch" was coined for exactly that: a person finds themself in an elevator with an investor or recruiter or prospect or someone else that they want to impress, and they have 30 seconds (the time you have a captive audience in the elevator) to make your pitch. You must take advantage of that opportunity, or it might be lost forever. The objective is clear, hopefully it will lead to a deeper discussion and further explanation of your specialty or product and ultimately result in a sale, funding, or some other clearly defined objective.

We may not even know it, but we find ourselves in these situations every single day. Whether it's at a deli, at the gym or at a friend's house, we are frequently faced with the question "So, what you do?" Just to be clear, that question does not give you a license to ramble on for 20 minutes about what you do. It is an invitation to talk for 30 seconds about your craft. Period.

While you only have 30 seconds, you still want a start with something that is emotionally charged, interesting and personal. Make that connection with them so they want you to "Tell them more." In a personal situation, it might be something as simple as "You know that thing you have on your counter in your kitchen? My company makes those, and I am the Director of Marketing." Well, that may be personal, but it is certainly not interesting and hardly emotional. More importantly, your introduction to a potential investor or recruiter must be interesting and connect on some emotional level. You must pique their interest to want to learn more. Typically, you start with a problem, and then follow that with your solution to the problem, briefly. You don't want to give away all the details especially when it includes some intellectual property and could violate some nondisclosure agreements. For example, talking to a potential investor, you can identify a problem that is causing a number of deaths per year and then say that your company has invented a product that will reduce those deaths by 75%. Always phrase the problem upfront in a way that the listener can connect to. The more emotional, the better, and saving lives is pretty emotional. If you happen to step on an elevator with the CEO of a company that you want to work for, you have very little time to convey to the CEO that you can increase sales, reduce expenses, improve productivity or increase profits, based on your experience, and include an example. Don't be afraid to ask for the follow up. It's better to get a "no" then let them get off the elevator without any answer.

Networking Group Introductions

Networking groups, including chambers, are a great way to practice your presentation skills, well at least your introduction. Most groups allow you one to two minutes to introduce yourself to the group and while that is not a lot of time it is the perfect opportunity to try out some of your introductions. This allows you to gauge the audience responses to see which introductions elicit the best response for the particular audience. Your objective in these meetings is to convince the group why they should refer you to their contacts. So how do you do that in one or two minutes? When you have very little time, you must keep in mind the concept of "Tell me more" and try to stay away from the "So What" or "Who Cares" responses. With so little time, every sound you make is critical and needs to be part of your strategy. As you speak each part of your introduction, you want your audience to respond, "Tell me more" and if you do not get that response, that means you are getting the opposite response which is "So What" or "Who Cares." You really want to avoid the "So What" or "Who Cares" responses.

The concept is simple. Start your introduction with something that is out of the ordinary to generate interest. This should be something that connects with the audience that makes them sit up and take notice and become ready to listen to the rest of your introduction. Then after you have their attention, tell them one more piece of information that builds off the first statement, maintaining the audience's interest level. Then you can close with your name and company and some instructions on how to follow up with you or what types of prospects you are looking to find.

When you are one of many people giving a 1–2-minute introduction, chances are the audience started to glaze over after the first couple of introductions. That is why you must stand out with something unexpected and different, otherwise your message will go unheard. You need to connect to the members of the group and anything that does not make that connection will receive a "So What" response. Many of these introductions start out with the person's name, the company name, what the company does, how big and great the company is, and what products and services the company offers. Using that type of approach will result in at least 5 "So What" or "Who cares" responses. There is not even one benefit or interesting morsel as to what the person can do or why the person should refer them. Let me use two examples for a weight loss professional with audience subconscious responses in parenthesis:

> "My name is Sally Smith (so what), and I worked for ABC Nutritional Company (so what). We are the largest nutritional products distributor in 3 continents (so what) and we provide nutritional products ranging from shakes to full meals (so what). We have won awards for our products (so what) and have excellent customer service (so what)."

Ouch, that was painful. She sounds just like XYZ Nutritional Company (if there is one). There was nothing unique, nothing interesting and nothing to get the audience's attention. The only person that might be interested in that company is someone looking for a job. Here is an alternative that emotionally engages the audience with audience subconscious responses in parenthesis:

> "Last month my clients lost over 600 lbs. (tell me more). I worked with them personally to monitor their progress along a personalized weight loss and nutrition plan (tell me more). We offer customize weight loss plans for individuals based on age, weight and lifestyle to assure success (tell me more, sounds expensive). We have plans for every budget and we guarantee our results (tell me more, how do I sign up?). To find out more,

meet me afterwards. My name is Sally Smith and the Company is ABC Nutritional Company."

Notice in the second example, it starts with an interesting statement that instantly captures the attention of the audience that makes them sit up and take notice and want to hear more. They think to themselves, "How did they lose 600 pounds? Is that 600 clients losing 1 pound each? That's not impressive. Is it 20 clients losing 30 pounds each? That's not healthy." So, they want to hear more. Then she elaborates about these customized plans which also sounds interesting to the audience who is already paying attention. But the customized plans sound expensive, so she then follows up with the plans and the guarantee. By the time she gets near the end, the audience is literally begging for her name and contact information.

If you want to guarantee a "So What" response, start with your name and company name, and how big or how long your company has been around. Boasting about the company does nothing to instill an emotional connection between you and the audience and the listing of products and services does nothing if you have not identified a need. Avoid starting with your name because if you only say it once, unless you are a famous actor/actress or sports figure, they will have no reason to remember it, as you have not made the connection yet. But if you make the connection with them, spark their interest enough to want to follow up, then when you tell them your name, they will be ready and willing to remember it.

Be creative. There is something that will connect you with the audience for every profession. You want to stand out from the others, especially if you are in a group with more than one person in your industry. Let me ask you this question. If you heard 3 financial advisors introduce themselves, with their name, company and the description that they offer a full range of financial products, but the fourth one started off by saying something like "Last year my clients' portfolios outperformed the market but 20%," which one would you want to follow up with?

Often these networking groups meet on a regular basis with many of the same people in the room. While this forum gives you the ability to practice your introduction, you can become comfortable and complacent in your delivery. Challenge yourself to make it more interesting every time without repeating the same exact thing. Incorporate recent news or events and make the connection. For example, if summer is coming our nutritional professional can reference the need for all of us to get trim to fit into our bikinis. Or near year end, financial advisors can throw out a tidbit of information on the amounts that can be saved with effective year-end tax planning. Keep it fresh, keep it interesting, be remembered, and you will get referrals.

Working the Tradeshow Booth

If you think a quick one-to-two-minute introduction is short, you have much less time to catch someone's attention working a tradeshow booth. You have between 3 and 5 seconds to catch someone's attention at a tradeshow before they pass by. There are some obvious things you can do to slow down the passersby (e.g., fishbowl raffle, pens and other marketing trinkets, and an impressive display) but you must have at least one quick teaser line that makes them stop dead in their tracks and say "Ok, Tell me more." Everyone's needs are different and tradeshow attendees usually encompass people with a wide range of needs. The most important thing is to define your target prospect before the show starts and make sure all your exhibitors are on the same page about the prospect. Know how to identify these prospects and what to say to get them to spend time learning about your offerings. Equally important is the ability to let go of someone that is clearly not interested and let them move on. Save your energy for others. Don't be like the solar panel salesperson that spends time with renters. I saw this at the mall. He had a pretty good introductory line about getting reduced utility expenses paid for by the government. The couple said no and said they rented. Instead of letting it go, the salesman got closer and then asked the couple for the name and phone number of their landlord. That made the couple very uncomfortable. The salesman should have just wished them a good day and looked for another prospect that met his predefine target prospects.

At a trade show booth, you don't have time to spend any time building up a story. You must launch a one liner at them as they approach, capture their interest, or let them move on. Remember to smile and appear warm, inviting and charming, otherwise your success rate will be low. If you are witty, funny and can think quickly on your feet, that is a big plus.

Be careful with your promotional materials and your actual tradeshow booth. You don't want your display to chase away your potential customers before you have a chance to toss out your catchy one liner. Typically, an accounting firm will proudly display their name on the booth and list their services, accounting, auditing, tax, etc. It's pretty boring. Another accounting firm in the same show had a booth that said, "Find out how to double your profits." Can you guess which booth had more visitors? Right, more people were curious about finding out how to double their profits then looking for a new accounting firm.

I was walking the streets of San Francisco one day and I passed by one homeless person after another, asking for money. I just ignored them. It was the same story repeatedly. It was very similar to some tradeshows I have attended, except the tradeshow people are usually standing. Then as I crossed the street one beggar shouted out, "How about twenty-five bucks so I can get a lobster dinner." I stopped dead in my tracks. He was different and stood out from all the others. He got me to stop and engage with him. When you are trying to create your teaser that stops the attendees in their tracks and wanting you to tell them more, keep this story in mind.

Online and Teleconference Presentations

Teleconferences are a great way to save on travel costs and ideal for training and education and presenting products to prospects. When there is a vested interest in the audience to actively participate and be on time, teleconferences can be very effective. However, teleconferences are not as effective for inspirational and motivational presentations. With 80% of communication being nonverbal, memorable inspirational teleconferences are especially difficult. As the speaker, it is difficult to determine if people are paying attention, actively listing, or have you on mute and conducting other business in their offices.

Delivering a presentation online can have its advantages and disadvantages. Depending on what you want to accomplish it can be good or not so good for your presentation. If you weigh the advantages against the disadvantages, you may find ways to mitigate the disadvantages to leverage into an advantage. Let's review.

Advantages of Online Presentations

1. **Increased Ability to Communicate** – With online meetings and presentations you have an increased ability to communicate to more people more often. There are no distance barriers to online communication. People from different time zones and different countries can participate in your meetings. Having online video meetings with people that normally would not meet in person improves their personal connection. The second part of this is that you can cover more in an online meeting in half the time, since you are eliminating the idle time of arrival, getting seated and normal in person delays. If you are giving a webinar there is a much better chance you can get someone to attend a 30- or 60-minute online webinar instead of trucking down to the local conference center, wasting half the day.

2. **Ubiquitous Access**. While it is difficult and costly to get people from disparate locations to meet in person to attend conferences, online meetings eliminate that problem. The key decision makers can make the meeting despite having busy schedules. Online meetings are more accessible than any other medium.

3. **Save Time.** Time is a very precious commodity. For success, one must be able to manage time effectively. The more efficient, the more productive, the more successful. Avoiding a business trip to hold a meeting is a huge time saver. Think about it. If you have an 8:30 am meeting, chances are people are arriving between 8:15 and 8:45 am. They spend time chatting with others, getting coffee, and getting situated (e.g., picking a seat). While interfacing with fellow workers is great for networking and brainstorming, it may also be an inefficient use of valuable time. Online meetings start on time and avoid the pre meeting idle time.

4. **Cost Savings** – Being able to conduct online meetings completely eliminates travel and other costs associated with gathering people altogether in one place. No more catered breakfast or lunches, no more travel costs, let alone being away from one's family, that is an intangible cost.

5. **Easier Access for Learning and Interaction.** When conducting online meetings, if the meeting is run correctly, it allows for all participants to express their views and participate in polls and questions. Often, for in-person meetings there may be hesitation for certain participants to comment. Online meetings often allow for interactive tools to quiz the participants to get instant responses to gauge understanding and buy-in. Or just to see if anyone is really paying attention.

6. **Better Form of Sharing Information** – Online meetings allow for all handouts and leave behinds to be available online as part of the presentation so hard copies do not need to be made, saving costs and trees. Meetings can be recorded and played back by participants if they need to review certain information that they may need to hear again. This accommodates users that are fast learners as well as those more methodical learners that need to review things more thoroughly to grasp the concepts.

7. **Ideal for Auditory and Visual learner types**. Speaking of different types of learners, with online presentations you must

provide a reason for the participants to focus, and this typically includes a PowerPoint and a dynamic speaker, hence appealing to both auditory and visual learners. Conference calls are great for auditory learners but can be difficult on visual learners. If you don't have interesting content to share on the screen and are not speaking with inflection and enthusiasm, you will have a difficult time maintaining audience focus online.

Those are some pretty powerful advantages, but before we get too excited, let's review some of the disadvantages.

Disadvantages of Online Presentations

1. **Less Direct Personal Contact.** Since 80% of communication is nonverbal, words alone cannot carry your message, which is why text and email can be confusing as to intent. However, an online meeting allows you to see a person's facial expressions and gauge what they are really saying. The problem is a face does not provide the full picture. To truly get to understand the message being delivered you must see the user's entire body. This means that with online meetings there is a chance that messages will still be misinterpreted.

2. **Poor Technology Reduces Effectiveness** – You can never rely on a consistent internet connection because it is just not possible in today's world. While the internet connection is mostly out of your control, there are some things you can do to make sure your technology is of high quality, so any disruption is not because of you. Never rely on your computer's microphone as it is low quality and tends to make you sound faint and weak. The lighting and background noise can also be a factor. Make sure the lighting on your face is good so you are not in the shadows and people can see your face. You don't want to look like you are in the witness protection program where users cannot see your face clearly. Try to eliminate all background noise by conducting your meeting in a room where it is expected to be quiet.

3. **Less Human Contact.** Humans thrive on social contact and interaction. Lost with online meetings is the social interactions that are so important to building relationships. Comradery among peers at work is lost when meetings and work is done online, which can have an impact on turnover, productivity and loyalty.

4. **Users Ability to Multitask** may mean they may not be focused on your presentation. Are they really listening? If you are making a presentation online there is the ability for participants to do other work instead of listening to you. It is possible to pull up another program on top of your online meeting window which makes it look like they are staring at your presentation, while they are really working on a sophisticated spreadsheet and have no idea what you are saying.

5. **Missed Introductions** – A great presentation starts with an intriguing introduction that lays the groundwork for the entire presentation. People that show up late to your online meeting may miss that important information and never really catch up. Typically, with inperson presentations, the meeting will start when all users have arrived.

6. **Ability to Be Hacked** – Is your meeting discussing top secret information? Be careful, hackers are out there and can hack into your meeting and steal your information. While security is getting better every day so are the hackers. Be careful what you share.
7. **Risk of Inadequate Planning** – while there is no room to book, no food to be catered and no microphone and podium to be ordered, there is still plenty of work to be done to organize an effective online meeting. There is the risk that other planning aspects may not be done as diligently and result in a poor presentation.

8. **Being Talked Over and Interrupted** – was cited by participants of online meetings as the number one complaint or challenge with online meetings. It is the job of the moderator to identify those that are trying to contribute and manage the interruptions, but that is often not so easy. With larger groups it becomes impossible for those that want to contribute to get their comments heard

Online meetings have advantages and disadvantages. Mostly, they are more cost effective and more efficient as well as convenient and more productive. However, they reduce the personal connections between participants and also increase connection between users from far away places. Be careful to plan effectively and weigh the pros and cons for each of your presentations.

Preparing your Online Presentation

When users are logging into your online meeting it is recommended that you have a waiting slide or video for them to watch while they are waiting for others to get online and the meeting to be started. It should not be your opening slide, but something that has more information. Maybe it can be some of the links or the preassigned reading or some related articles for the topic to be discussed. An even better alternative is to have the speaker available for casual conversation and questions before the meeting starts. It can be an open forum welcoming people to the meeting and getting them relaxed and prepared for an awesome presentation.

When you start your meeting, give them your introduction. This introduction is really no different from a standard in-person introduction, but just keep in mind that you have an extra level of interest that must be maintained online.

It is very important to tell your audience the allotment of time. Tell them that the presentation is set for say 20 minutes and have allowed 10 minutes for questions. This gives them a frame of reference to know how much time to devote to this presentation. If you don't tell them how long you will be presenting, they may be distracted as emails come into their inbox, instead of focusing on you and waiting for the planned break to respond to emails. For longer meetings that may span several hours, it is courteous to let them know when the breaks will be so they can plan accordingly. Your agenda, if you have one, should show the times allocated to each section of the presentation throughout the day with times for lunch and coffee breaks identified specifically in the agenda. It is courteous to tell the audience in the longer meetings how long the next section will be. For example, for the next 90 minute we will be reviewing the sales pipeline and tracking enhancements.

Also, tell them in your introduction that you will provide links to various sources of information that is used in the presentation. These links will be available during and after the presentation.

When you are online, less of the presentation is you and more is what content you are displaying on the screen. In person, you have your entire body moving around and attracting attention and being animated to keep them engaged. Online you do not have that. When I am in person, I move around the floor to force the audience to move their eyes and their head to follow me. That is not possible with online presentations. The content of what you are presenting, your enthusiasm and your entertaining voice is what has to keep them engaged, which is a little more challenging. For these reasons you must use high impact content and images. Use short bullets and one-word slides for impact.

As you go through your slides, include links to the information on screen and put the links in the chat window so they can participate by downloading it in real time and read along with you.

Remember to include some interactivity. When they are online, they are probably sitting in a comfortable chair staring at their screen. How long can they do that without some stimulation? Incorporate some interactivity, frequently. Ask them questions that require a response in the chat box. The first question is "Can everyone hear me." Type "Yes" if you can hear me." Then as you go on with your content you can ask for specific answers in the chat, as well. Use polls and surveys to gather information in real time to certain questions. Consider using break out groups to allow specific people to work together on specific problems. Randomly call on people for specific answers to questions. Keep them engaged.

The keys to consider in online presentations are that at any point they can click you off. You want to avoid that, of course, but keep them to the end and give them a reason to act on your call to action. If you want them to sign up for something, give them a discount, or a freebie or another incentive to get to your objective. There is no way to talk to each one as they walk out the door, because they are a click away from being gone.

I believe the most difficult thing in a teleconference or online presentation is maintaining energy. I personally get more energy the more I sense the interest of the audience, mostly by looking at their faces or fielding their questions. This excited me. Without the ability to see the audience's faces or even determine if they are watching their computer screen, the energy level can drop. With an energy drop comes less inflection in your voice. You must manufacture energy, imagine the audience is giving you positive feedback and avoid the monotone slide.

Tips for Presenting Online

2020 will forever be known as the year that business meetings went online. Online meetings increased over 50% with the onset of the COVID 19 pandemic. This came on suddenly and meetings were immediately shifted to online without any real training on how to present online. It is different and must be approached differently.

Whether you are a participant or the meeting moderator, there are simple things you can do the make sure you promote a professional image. You cannot control the occasional siren or garbage truck noise rumbling down the street, but you can control the following items that will have a positive impact on your image. You don't want to lose a potential sale because you don't present as a professional.

Professional Platform. Choose a professional platform for conducting your meetings. There are many good ones, and they are not expensive. Screen sharing, video conference, chat boxes, login and registration so you can control who gets on and know who is really connected and attending your meeting. Most of these platforms offer a polling feature that is good for soliciting feedback from participants to keep them involved in the meeting.

Designated Separate Space – When you conduct your online meetings make sure your workspace looks like a workspace and not a kitchen. The room you work in and conduct your meetings should be carpeted and have furniture in it. This helps with the acoustics and reduces echo. An echo or hollow sound in your room is not good when having online meetings.

Proper Lighting – Improper lighting can make you look unprofessional and low tech. I often see people online with the sun or bright lights behind them, making their faces dark. Another issue can arise if your camera does not do well in low light. To make sure you have adequate lighting do these 3 things:

1. Check your background and make sure you have adequate lighting on your face and there is nothing bright behind you.
2. Invest in a better external camera to raise your professionalism.
3. If you want to look younger and fresher, put a light below your head to lighten up the space underneath your eyes. You can also use a light-colored desk that reflects the light in a similar manner.

Virtual Backgrounds - Many home offices are located in kitchens, dining rooms or bedrooms. If this is you and you still want to look professional, you should consider using a virtual background. On Zoom you can click on settings, then backgrounds and filters and choose one of the standard backgrounds or add new ones. You can search the internet for virtual backgrounds for Zoom meetings and find ones that you like. Other meeting platforms do not allow for virtual backgrounds so take care that what is behind you is not embarrassing. Be careful because there are some pretty crazy backgrounds you can use, so pick one that will raise your professional image and not detract from it. Alternatively, you can create your own background. Some I have seen are an image of the lobby or conference room and then super imposed on the background is the company's logo, making it look like you are in the office. A nice touch. Stay away from backgrounds that show you at the beach or on vacation.

Proper Acoustics – Similar to lighting, having proper sound and acoustics is key for promoting a professional image. Do not rely on your computers built-in microphone. It will make you sound faint and weak. Invest in an external microphone to improve the tone and voice. If you invest in a professional microphone, you can be assured you sound professional and confident.

Test Your Technical Equipment. Always test your microphone, camera and lighting before you start your meeting. Sometimes your computer processes some system updates and may turn off a driver overnight so your camera or microphone may not work, even though it worked the day before. To be sure, set up a test meeting to make sure everything is working properly. You can never predict the unexpected when it comes to technology, but testing your equipment will give you confidence and assurance your presentation will go well.

Camera at Eye Level – If you are using a laptop on the desk and it is below your head, the angle of the camera will not be a flattering one. Get your camera at the same height as your eyes. This will provide a picture of your face that is not distorted and more natural.

Look Directly at the Camera to Make a Point – This is actually very difficult, since all the other participants are on your screen, which is below the integrated camera. If you are speaking and you want to accentuate a point, stare directly at the camera, not the faces of the participants. To make this easier to do, you can use an external camera and put it directly in front of the faces on the screen.

Consider Standing if You Will Be Speaking – Your voice projects better when you stand then when you are seated. You come across more professional. The issue with standing is that people tend to rock or move around which is distracting when online. If you sit up straight your diaphragm will be able to process air more freely and your voice will sound better.

Turn Off Your Other Devices – This includes your desk phone as well as your mobile devices and any other device that may make noise during your meeting. Try to minimize other noises that might crop up. If you have a dog for example, take the dog for a walk before your meeting so he will be sleeping during your call. If you are expecting FedEx or UPS Delivery, when you hear the truck, mute yourself when they come up to the door to ring the bell.

Dress Properly – Working at home has its advantages especially when it comes to attire. However, when you have a meeting, take care to dress appropriately for the audience, at least above the waist.

Use Multiple Screens – Use multiple screens to increase your proficiency. You can have your notes on one screen and your presentation on the other. If there is an issue or a question that you need to answer while you are sharing your main screen, you can also look up the answer on the second screen without disrupting the main screen. When using PowerPoint or another presentation software with multiple screens, when you share your screen, the audience sees the full slide and you see both the slide, the slide notes and the next slide or click action in the sequence. This is very handy.

Sticky Notes – The really nice thing about presenting online is that you can have all kinds of notes handy to assist you that you would not necessarily have when you are in front of an audience. One option, besides a note pad on your desk and a document on your second screen is to put skicky notes around the screen with your camera. These sticky notes are good for reminders, like remember to smile, your call to action, points to repeat, etc. These are great because it does not take your head or eyes away from the screen.

Remember since the pandemic there has been a 50% increase in the number of online virtual meetings and that number is expected to continue to grow.

15. IN SUMMARY

"Make sure you have stopped speaking before your audience has stopped listening." – Dorothy Sarnoff

When making a presentation, put yourself in the audience's shoes. Ask yourself what you would like to hear and see, and how you would want to hear and see it. Would you like to be an active participant or a passive listener? Would you like to be forced to stay at one group learning level or be allowed to learn at your own level? Would you want a monotone lecture by someone behind a podium using more than ten slides per minute, or would you like to be an active participant in an interesting story, a magical journey, watch and listen to someone who moves around, using strong body language and a select group of slides to reinforce points for impact? Would you like to walk away from the presentation with a solid understanding of its purpose, or would you like to be unsure of why you even attended? Would you like to have a positive memory of the speaker? Would you like to leave on time? Would you like to feel that the speaker is current on the topic or would you like to hear a canned, stale presentation watered down to fit any audience? Would you like a speaker that is sympathetic to your needs and interests, or would you like the speaker to talk down to you or talk over your head? Would you want to be inspired and informed and glad you attended?

Incorporating the answers to the above questions into your next presentation will make all the difference. Whatever your situation, whatever your audience, be prepared to connect with them, tell them a story, get them to want you to "Tell them more," and take them on that magical journey.

Good luck and remember to have fun!

EXHIBIT I: PRESENTATION CHEAT SHEET

Theme	Develop your overriding theme that will tie everything together and be the main point your audience will remember about you.
The Journey	Define the magical journey that your presentation will take your audience through during your presentation
Introduction	Create an introduction that connects with your audience that makes them eager to learn more about what you have to say and subconsciously think "Tell me more."
Content	Create the content blocks of information that support your theme and take your audience along their journey (a.k.a. your presentation)
Visual Aids	Create Eye-catching visual aids to support and enhance your presentation.
Call to Action	Determine what you want your audience to do as a result of hearing your presentation.

EXHIBIT II: TOP THINGS TO GUARANTEE FAILURE

1. Apologize for anything including being boring, being nervous or being unprepared.
2. Be unprepared.
3. Don't have a consistent theme.
4. Creating your slides first before you define your theme and your content.
5. Start with an old joke.
6. Read your speech from sheets of paper from a podium.
7. Speak without enthusiasm, in a monotone or quiet voice.
8. Deliver a speech from memorization without emotion or inflection.
9. Walk about the room without purpose.
10. Stand in one place and rock back and forth or use gestures or motions that are not intentional or relevant to the presentation.
11. Dress unprofessionally or inappropriate for the audience.
12. Talk about how great you are – bragging.
13. Speak to your screen with your back to the audience.
14. Run over your allotted presentation time.
15. Use a lot of acronyms that make you sound smart.
16. Use fact and figures that are unverified.
17. Mispronounce words, phrases or names that the audience knows well.
18. Fail to give your audience an action for follow-up.
19. Forget to personalize your presentation.

EXHIBIT III: FIVE POINT SLIDE CHECKLIST

1. Does it emotionally engage your audience?
2. Is it understandable as to readability (text) and the point of the slide?
3. Is it creative and interesting, as well as aesthetically pleasing?
4. Is it part of the story that are trying convey?
5. Does the slide create interest in the audience to learn more about your topic?

EXHIBIT IV: PRE-EVENT CHECKLIST

1. CONTENT
    - What is your main overriding theme?
    - Are your calls to action clearly identifiable?
    - Have you practiced enough?
    - Are you slides readable and do they support your objective?
    - Do you have enough copies of your hand outs?
    - Have you uploaded your deliverables to a website link that the audience can download?
    - Do you have a back up copies of your presentation on a flash drive?
    - Do you have a slightly longer and shorter presentation version in case you are asked to adjust your time?
2. LOGISTICS
    - Does you agenda have times listed?
    - Have you tested the projector if you are using one?
    - Did you survey the room to make sure it accommodates your style?
    - Do you have a microphone? Do you need one?
    - If you plan to use flipcharts, will the walls in the room support taping them up?
    - Have you coordinated with other speakers at the event?
3. PERSONAL
    - Do you remember that you are the expert and that is why you are speaking?
    - Did you eat the appropriate non spicy foods the night before and the morning of your speech?
    - Are you ready to be successful?

Made in the USA
Columbia, SC
25 April 2024